The Exposure of Luxury

BARBARA HARDY

The Exposure of Luxury

Radical Themes
in Thackeray

UNIVERSITY OF PITTSBURGH PRESS

First published in England 1972 by
Peter Owen Ltd

ISBN 0-8229-1104-3

Library of Congress Catalog Card Number 75-185025
Manufactured in Great Britain

TO BILL

CONTENTS

ILLUSTRATIONS

The illustrations in this volume taken from *Vanity Fair* and *Pendennis* are by W. M. Thackeray; those from *The Newcomes* are by Richard Doyle; and the illustration from *Lovel the Widower* is by Harry Furniss:

Vanity Fair: pages 6, 10, 124 and tail-piece; *Pendennis*: pages 40 ('Mr Morgan at His Ease'), 65 and 89; *The Newcomes*: pages 115, 148, 154 ('To Be Sold'), and 176 ('At the Hôtel de Florac'); *Lovel the Widower*: page 81 ('The Mother Syrens').

The photograph on the dust-jacket, of Bronzino's painting *The Exposure of Luxury*, is reproduced by courtesy of the National Gallery, London.

ACKNOWLEDGEMENTS

My debt to Gordon N. Ray's biographies, *Thackeray: The Uses of Adversity* (1955) and *Thackeray: The Age of Wisdom* (1958), and to his edition of *The Letters and Private Papers of William Makepeace Thackeray* (1945-6), will be plain, and I am grateful to Mrs Belinda Norman Butler, Dr Ray and to Harvard University for permission to quote from the biographies and *The Letters*.

I should like to thank Laurel Brake and Jennifer Chisman for their hard work and patience, Michael Levien for his careful reading of the manuscript and for suggestions, and the following people for encouragement and help : Benjamin DeMott, Julia and Kate Hardy, Samuel Hynes, Peter Owen, and the members of my graduate seminar on *Vanity Fair* at Birkbeck College.

B.H.

Introduction

'I have no head above my eyes.'[1]
Thackeray

Coming to the study of Thackeray from George Eliot and Dickens, two other great Victorian novelists, I was at first struck by apparently unrelated things: his comic self-consciousness as an artist, very much closer to the eighteenth- than to the nineteenth-century novelist, and his explicit refusal to use fiction for high moral triumphs. The self-consciousness and the lack of moral optimism, I now believe, are closely related to each other as aspects of his radical thinking and caring about humanity. Thackeray has frequently been accused of cynicism and pessimism, probably less because he is so critical of society, than because he offers neither the humane meliorism of George Eliot, nor the quasi-Christian optimism of Dickens, nor the tragic sublimities of Thomas Hardy. George Eliot used her novels to show the potentialities of human nature, and their implications for a social faith; Dickens made a more radical criticism of society and a purer and more abstract presentation of transcendent human virtue; Hardy saw both nature and society as traps for the creative man, but affirmed the nobility of his defeated heroes and heroines. George Eliot is a greater psychological realist than Dickens, but their conclusions are close, both taking a critical view of society, a critical view of socially determined human weakness, but a more or less hopeful view – more in Dickens, less in George Eliot – of individual love, creativity and progress. This hopefulness gives their very different novels the

[1] Thackeray said this in conversation with the American journalist George William Curtis. It is quoted by Ray in *Life*, Vol. 2, p. 119.

common feature which we seldom find in Thackeray: the creation of uncriticized characters. Their insistence on the possible emergence from aggression and acquisitiveness creates the portraiture of virtue, as an act of faith, as for instance in the testimonies implicit or explicit in Agnes, Nell, Dorrit, Joe and Biddy, Dinah Morris, Adam Bede, Felix Holt, Dorothea and Daniel Deronda. George Eliot is a psychological realist who recreates, as Dickens in his symbolic stereotyping does not, the complexities of love, but they both use action and character to represent creativity, unselfishness and love. Thackeray's art and vision are very different.

When readers complained about Thackeray's cynicism, such constructive images of virtue were very likely what they missed.[2] Their absence is certainly depressing to most readers, and must have been particularly so in a socially restless and very Christian period like the post-Reform Act England of the 1840s and 1850s. What Thackeray wanted to do, he explained[3] apropos the decidedly muted ending of *Vanity Fair*, was to make us dissatisfied. Dissatisfaction is far from a tragic response, and Thackeray's pessimism is nothing like as heartening as Hardy's, or even Gissing's. With the exception of *Henry Esmond*, the novel of 'cut-throat melancholy', his novels are comic novels, and he is an uncomfortable writer, apparently believing in neither stoicism or baptisms of suffering, and, while not dissenting from Christianity, offering no religious solutions. George Eliot was even less Christian, finally rejecting both the Old and the New Testaments whereas Thackeray rejected only the Old, but her crisis of faith left her with a fervent Feuerbachian surrogate for religion – a belief in Duty.

Thackeray seems not to have undergone any crisis of faith, and his religion sits very lightly on him. If occasionally he shows a Helen or Laura Pendennis possessed of a religious faith and piety that awe the average sensual hero like Arthur Pendennis, such characters draw attention to the absence of embodied religious feeling in the novels. The religious moments in Thackeray either have a veil drawn over them, which has the effect of a neutral reticence rather than a sacred awe, or are handled rather

---

[2] They were accustomed to finding them in Fielding, Richardson and Dickens, among the great novelists.

[3] *Letters*, Vol. II, p. 423.

sanctimoniously, as with the last days of Colonel Newcome in Charterhouse. What Thackeray's beliefs were, and what he implied in such reticence or excess, is less important than the existence of a social criticism and moral action in art which seems to depend no more than George Eliot's morality on any conception of 'what is not human'.

Thackeray is, then, neither a comforting Christian, nor an agnostic optimist, nor a strongly humane pessimist. The result is not heartening, and may have something to do with his relative neglect. People still read *Vanity Fair* and *Esmond*, but judging by the testimonies of students and acquaintances, hardly anyone now reads *Pendennis* and *The Newcomes* (two very great novels indeed), and most people have never even heard of *A Shabby Genteel Story* or *The Adventures of Philip*. Writing about Thackeray is very different from writing about George Eliot or Dickens: it seems impossible to take for granted either the extent or the depth of knowledge which one can assume about the other two writers, and so I have more or less limited my discussion to the four major novels, *Vanity Fair*, *Pendennis*, *Esmond* and *The Newcomes*. I have also been lavish with quotation and summary of action, not only in the hope of making my case, but of letting Thackeray speak for himself.

I have been the readier to do this because my subject is first and foremost his content, and only indirectly his form. I came to the study of Thackeray from a general interest in the aesthetics of fiction, but found myself drawn less by Thackeray's techniques than by his subject-matter. Indeed, I think that the content of his novels has been oddly neglected, certainly in the case of the major social themes. There has always been interest in the themes and thought of George Eliot, but until some twelve years ago there was very little detailed work on her powers as an artist. Thackeray, on the other hand, has for some time past attracted aesthetic discussion and formal analysis, but there still seems to be plenty of room for a discussion of his central subjects. My book is not a general and comprehensive study of Thackeray's themes, but attempts to point to some aspects of his social criticism. Although I work largely through a discussion of the themes, I am also, indirectly, but I hope emphatically, concerned with their embodiment in the forms of fiction. The themes I discuss seem to me to be at the heart of the four major

novels, *Vanity Fair, Pendennis, Esmond* and *The Newcomes.*
They are : rank, class, trade, commerce, money, insincerity and
artifice, the corruptions of hospitality, fellowship and love. I have
selected from these themes a group of subjects which show
Thackeray's preoccupation with the surface manners and con-
duct of 'his' society, whether it is the England of Queen Anne,
the Regency, Waterloo, or the contemporary 1840s and 1850s.
The relationships of rank and class are shown most strikingly in
scenes of confrontation and reversal. The dramatized debate
between nature and art, closely related to the idea of profitable
acts and performance, pervades characterization, action and
symbolism. The corrupt relations and values shown in object-
worship and conspicuous consumption perversely animate description and scene. The travesty of harmony and relationship
shown in Thackeray's favourite occasions – feasts, parties and
ceremonies – shapes scene after scene, and symbol after symbol.
I have, in conclusion, said something about the theme implied
negatively in all these critical exposures – Love. While my reading of Thackeray has led me to assert most confidently that he
has no cheering moral triumphs or inspiring tragic failures, it is
still true that in his muted, moderate and realistic vision there
is some little room for certain attempts at loving.

Thackeray is a highly rational and realistic artist, and his
excessive rationality may have led him to avoid visionary suggestions or symbols of love and creativity. His hopes are pitched
very low, but their presence is immensely important, acting as
assurance of his warmth and generosity (despite the satirist's and
the joker's stance) and as a sign of the fierce and feeling heart at
the centre of his social analysis. Dickens worked out a brilliant
imaginative resource for showing the pressures of society on the
generous and creative spirit by imagining split characters, like
Jaggers and Wemmick in *Great Expectations,* whose duality
suggests and explores both the possibilities of social perversion
and the resistance put up by imagination and love. It is these
dual characters, rather than Dickens's angelic women and children, who make most plain his attack on a crazily unjust society.
Thackeray avoids such melodramatically split characters, but he
is perhaps attempting something similar in his mixed and
ironically presented good characters, all at their best only fairly
good – Amelia, Dobbin, Rawdon, Pen, Henry Esmond, Rachel

Castlewood, Clive, Ethel, and Colonel Newcome. They are all criticized and they are all more wholly involved in *Vanity Fair* than Dickens's compartmentalized people ever are, more heavily committed to its values and ways of life. There is also a significant absence in Thackeray of mouthpiece-characters; with the possible exception of Laura Pendennis and Warrington no one mounts a systematic attack or even puts forward a radical question about social morality, like Paul Dombey, Little Dorrit or Esther Summerson. Not only does Thackeray create no virtuous characters, and no intact virtues within characters, but he has no radical critics.

It is often argued that Thackeray was a conservative in social attitudes, despite his interest in Liberal politics, his unsuccessful attempt to stand for Parliament and his associations with Reform. Certainly much that he said and did seems to show an acceptance, if not a total liking, for society as he found it, as in this draft of a speech which was intended[4] for a meeting of the Administrative Reform Society:

> If all of us here happened to be Earls or let us say the eldest sons of Earls with a prospect of a seat in yonder begilt and befrescoed hall at Westminster on the lamented demise of the noble peers our Fathers, we should be naturally hostile to the proceedings of certain agitators out of doors – as I believe & am sure our friends of Westminster are. Why gentlemen if we had hereditary seats in this theatre comfortable wadded stalls in w^h we and our descendants might sit forever and see the opera for nothing we should be peevish I daresay and object to changes of a system w^h worked very well and made us very comfortable. We should like to have our relatives and our friends with good room in the pit our wives and daughters with good boxes and our flunkies up in the galleries – It is but human nature; and I am disposed to look not quite so angrily as some gentlemen here at the conduct of our governing classes and governors – at their dislike to this association at their testy rage, at their high & mighty contempt at w^h we can afford to laugh, at their jokes too. . . . (*Letters*, Vol. III, pp. 683-4)

My contention in this book is Lawrence's 'never trust the artist, trust the tale'. To say it another way, and more precisely:

4 It was never made.

never trust the man at ease, living empirically the moment-to-moment life, participating appetitively in experience. Trust rather the book, the experience, the accumulation of social images and facts, the sheer weight of observation, shaped by drama, picture and psychology, compelling an imaginative unity not wholly within conscious control.

Thackeray was a journalist and a graphic artist, and his acute and precise presentation of the dense details of social surfaces, institutions, appearances, customs, objects, all graded, classed, placed, timed and priced, makes his novels much more socially informative than the work of more profound artists like Dickens and George Eliot. They *are* more profound, mining depths of the human mind and heart, and showing agonies, joys and creativity which hardly ever come into the world of Thackeray. I say 'hardly ever' because Henry Esmond's insight into the process of creative self-discovery in expression, whether of the artist or the imaginative man, with the closely related insight into the processes of feeling and memory, shows Thackeray's imagination sensitively active in ways not represented in his three great social novels. *Vanity Fair, Pendennis* and *The Newcomes.* But these insights and explorations are exceptions in Thackeray, and one would not go to his social novels for revelations about passion, endurance, joy, creation, faith, imagination. However, his usual limitation has its special virtue. His brilliant understanding of the surface, and his abstention from systematic criticism and voiced social ethic, allow society to show itself, astounding, mad, hollow, frightening.

He does not make a passive record. He is a critic, a clown, a satirist, a preacher, but his actual preaching and his eloquent irony about society, seen magnificently in such set-pieces as the analysis of Sir Pitt Crawley, or the two chapters in *Vanity Fair,* 'How to Live Well on Nothing A-Year', while incisive, are accompanied by a portrait that is far more eloquent, dramatized and indirect. Society's excessive and loveless occasions and ceremonies, its artificiality and shams, its pursuit of profit, its transformation of life into traffic and commodity, all reveal themselves unmistakably in a detached and eloquent self-exposure. The humour, tolerance and ease of Thackeray's comments on his social and personal experience in his letters, are replaced in his fiction by a shaped exposure of a cruel, cold, mad world.

There are a few things to notice about the forms of this social 'self-exposure'. It contains but also moves beyond Thackeray's explicit moral commentary, and it is often much more strongly emotional than the commentary itself. Thackeray as preacher in motley, one of his favourite authorial roles, is usually ironic, amused, affectionate, rational, well balanced. Thackeray as dramatist, showing rather than telling, or showing as well as telling, creates scenes which appeal to the sense of justice, the sense of moderation, the sense of generosity, even the sense of restrained pleasure. But his fierceness of attack on injustice and indeed his sense of the values of love and justice emerge through the collection of social facts and surfaces. Feasts, ostentatious displays, ceremonies, costumes, objects, cosmetics, masks, acts, strokes of wit go far beyond his rational appeals, analysis and commentary, to move us, dazzle us, disgust us, horrify us. For example : he never actually says that stratification of human relations by rank, class and title is absurd, and there is indeed no evidence outside the novels that he found it so. He enjoyed being taken up by the 'great world' as he became successful, and although he could laugh at the *bo-monde's* apparent disapproval of his lecture on George IV, he speaks tolerantly, if a little self-consciously, about the decency and simplicity of his aristocratic acquaintances. He was certainly no egalitarian, and some of his attitudes to race, for instance, are a serious embarrassment to his present-day admirers : they mostly appear in his letters from America, but sometimes within the novels too, in the decidedly unpleasant portraits of Miss Swartz in *Vanity Fair* and Mr Woolcomb in *Philip*. Nevertheless, in his presentation of human relations, he repeats situations in which power and class figure, and repeats a drama of disruption, collapse and reversal. In the scenes of power-relationships, and in the scenes of rebellion against that power, there gradually accretes a sense of the absurdity and injustice of such structuring of human relations. In life he engaged servants,[5] admired objects, gave and received presents, bought books, prints, clothes, furniture, food and drink, with a careful sense of investment, profit, appreciation and enjoyment. In his fiction there is very little innocent enjoyment of the pleasures of wining and dining, because they are presented

---

[5] There are many examples of his generosity and sympathy to servants.

in an accumulation of images and scenes, as a ridiculous, strategical, or excessive expenditure, as display. He creates a social surface which is an encrustation on human life, falsifying, enclosing, hardening, and destroying.

Not all the themes are so embedded in drama, or so dependent on the accumulations and repetitions. The contrast between the natural and the studied, the sincere and the plagiarized or performed existence, is made very explicit. But it is in the local scenes that the radicalism of argument is found. Every part of human life, every emotional act, is seen as tarnished or stemming twistedly from the greed (even in Amelia and Dobbin), the competition (even in Laura, Helen and Rachel) and the pursuit of goods and profits (even in Colonel Newcome). What emerges is the disgust or ironic pointing of sheer excess, dishonesty and lovelessness.

Thackeray does not always support drama with commentary, and he also frequently avoids the appeals and arguments of contrast. Riches, gain and snobbishness make their way in the novels, and make themselves felt by over-exposure and accumulation. When Dickens wants to show the unctuousness of a Chadband in *Bleak House,* he contrasts his periodic excess of language with the brief, broken words of the barely articulate Jo, his gluttony with Guster's crust, his condescension with Snagsby's apologetic kind giving. When George Eliot wants to show the vanity of Hetty Sorrel in *Adam Bede,* she shows her preening before her tarnished mirror, decked in shoddy but gaudy garments, in strong contrast with Dinah Morris's Quaker simplicity and outward gaze. In *Middlemarch* she sets Rosamond Vincy's elaborate clothing, conscious turn of neck and wondrous flaxen plaits against Dorothea's simplicity and unselfconsciousness. Although Thackeray uses the central contrast of Becky and Amelia in *Vanity Fair*, it turns out to be a very sly one, making us see resemblances where we had begun to expect only differences. It is, moreover, the only major contrast of this kind that he makes. His method is unlike that of the other Victorian novelists – George Eliot, Dickens, Trollope, Meredith, Henry James – who make extreme use of the polarity, the antithesis, the sheep-and-goat division. Thackeray does not divide human nature in this way, and it may well be that he used the grand comparative method for the first and last time in *Vanity*

Fair, perhaps discovering through and in the writing that what was clearer than the opposition between vice and virtue was a generalized, common pressure from society. Idolatry links even Amelia with the false gods of Vanity Fair, and even Dobbin has his vanities. But whatever the reason, Thackeray exhausted the device of contrast in this novel, and in the later ones it is absent. Pendennis, Henry Esmond, Clive Newcome and his father, are also strongly bent by their society.

The result, if we scrutinize it, is a radical criticism, even at times a radical despair. Gordon Ray describes Thackeray's political views as far from radical:

> The general feud between gentlemen and Bohemians, reinforced as it was by his personal quarrel with Dickens, substantially affected the political opinions that Thackeray entertained during his later years. Though his alliance with the Administrative Reform Association caused him for a time to abandon his political quietism for a moderate liberalism, this conversion was not lasting. After the Garrick Club affair Thackeray's controlling political principle was not suspense of judgment, as it had been in the early 1850s, but actual conservatism. He was reconciled to 'the Ornamental Classes', he wrote in a *Roundabout* paper. 'I like my lord mayor to have a gilt coach, my magnificent monarch to be surrounded by magnificent nobles.' In 1861 he accepted an essay for the *Cornhill Magazine* from James Fitzjames Stephen, which anticipates many of the points in that author's forcible polemic against liberalism and popular government in his *Liberty, Equality, Fraternity* of 1873. When its boldness alarmed George Smith, Thackeray argued: 'The article is a very moderate sensible plea for an aristocratic government, and shows the dangers of a democracy quite fairly. . . . The politics of gentlemen are pretty much alike. Since 48 in France, and especially since America I for one am very much inclined to subscribe to Stephen's article.' (*Life*, Vol. 2, pp. 312-13)

I am dissenting from Ray's emphasis, but I can see why he makes it. The evidence of the biography and the evidence of the fiction are two startlingly different things. Although I have spoken of Thackeray as possessing an exceptionally rational imagination, he did of course, like all great artists, reveal more than he consciously set out to reveal, perhaps indeed more than he knew or more than he knew he knew. Although he was a most conservative liberal, his novels work through report, locally imagined individual case, and accreted unity, to make what is to my mind one of the most revolutionary statements in the Victorian novel. I should make it clear that by 'revolutionary' I do not refer to doctrines or programmes of political revolt, but to revolutionary feeling. When Thackeray shows the polite and cultivated circle, we are as far as we could possibly be from Virginia Woolf's Mrs Ramsay and her dinner-party with the *Boeuf en Daube*. When he describes the beautiful object, it is like none of the Spoils of Poynton. When he depicts the pleasures and charms of wealth, it is not to praise them like Hyacinth Robinson in *The Princess Casamassima*. The feast, the object, and the delight compel a radical disgust, rejection or despair. His art emerges as most rational when least conscious. It is also most sane when what it displays is most absurd.

Thackeray's symbolism is frequently what I want to call a *literal* or *external* symbolism. It consists of symbols which already exist as facts of life : the meal, the house, the party, the polite address, the present, the entertainment, the song, the dance and the play. Thackeray is a most careful and intricate artist and his symbolic structure reflects his care and intricacy,[6] but I believe that his symbols are most effectively eloquent of radical feeling when they are not inventions of art but reports on life. Thackeray is the great sociologist of nineteenth-century fiction, the great accumulator of social symbols of class and money. To read him is to read a fictional form of Veblen's *The Theory of the Leisure Class*, or Marcel Mauss's *Essai sur le Don*, or Galbraith's *The Affluent Society*. Like these eloquent social scientists, he is not merely reporting or describing. Certain facts, if gathered together, unified, and shown in vivid particularity, create a statement of horror, disgust, incredulity. This is what Thackeray's portrait of conspicuous consumption, mercenary marriage and self-indulgence creates. But unlike the sociologist, he works through particularity. He is a great psychologist too, and the social

---

[6] As has been shown by several critics, particularly John Loofbourow, *Thackeray and the Form of Fiction* (Princeton, N. J.: Princeton University Press, 1964); James Wheatley, *Patterns in Thackeray's Fiction* (Cambridge, Mass.: MIT Press, 1969); Jean Sudrann, ' "The Philosopher's Property" ': Thackeray and the Use of Time', *VS*, 10 (June 1967), 359-88; and Henri Talon, 'Time and Memory in *Henry Esmond*', *RES*, 13 (May 1962), 147-56.

particularities – vivid sensuous and visual pictures of drawing-rooms, dining-rooms, meals, clothes, houses, streets, servants – are shown as the environment which creates, moulds, corrupts and restricts people and their relationships. As a critic of society, if we take him only at the face value of his explicit attacks, and of his conspicuous jokes, we will find him fervent, witty, sharp, but limited in range and depth. But if we attend to his implicit, as well as his explicit, analysis, we see his full range and depth of attack. And we see more. He shows what society is doing to people, perverting, crippling, and killing their capacity for love. He is radical in the way of his great ancestors in moral satire, Juvenal, Bunyan, Swift, Johnson, and in his most profound and central themes he reveals and criticizes the profound and central corruptions of Victorian society.[7]

[7] A. E. Dyson, in one of the very best articles on Thackeray's social criticism, 'Vanity Fair: An Irony against Heroes', *Critical Quarterly*, 6 (Spring 1964), attributes Thackeray's not wholly intentional radicalism to the 'intensity with which he always responded to the human comedy'.

Abbreviations used in footnotes :

NCF	=	*Nineteenth Century Fiction*
PMLA	=	*Publications of the Modern Language Association*
RES	=	*Review of English Studies*
VS	=	*Victorian Studies*

CHAPTER ONE

Rank and Reversal

The rank is but the guinea's stamp,
The man's the gowd for a' that.
>   Robert Burns, 'For A' That, An' A' That'

Take but degree away, untune that string,
And hark, what discord follows !
>   *Troilus and Cressida,* I, iii

Upper and Lower, Richer and Poorer, Master and Man, Husband and Wife, Rogue and Gull, Prince and Subject, Elder and Younger, Mentor and Pupil: these are some of the social, political and familial pairs into which Thackeray, through social analysis and with dramatic sensibility, groups his characters. To my mind, one source of critical uneasiness[1] about Thackeray's handling of big scenes like the discovery scene in *Vanity Fair* is the separation of Thackeray's art from his social analysis. But I believe his sense of theatre is intricately connected with his classification of social and psychological relations, which he tends to see as part of a power-structure involving class and possessions. He tends also to take great pleasure in the way the social relation works with and also against psychological relations, and such pleasure shows itself in his portrayal of reversals in relationships. At times the reversal involves an insight about particular people in a particular relation to each other, for this is of course fiction, not social typology. But the reversal always concerns a sense

---

[1] Among the critics who lack confidence in Thackeray's handling of the big dramatic scene is Percy Lubbock who set the tone for such apologies when he wrote his celebrated judgment on Thackeray's 'perversity': '. . . how little Thackeray's fashion of handling a novel allowed for the big dramatic scene, when at length it had to be faced – how he neglected it in advance, how he refused it till the last possible moment'. (*The Craft of Fiction,* London: Jonathan Cape, 1921) Even Kathleen Tillotson feels constrained to talk about the element of parody in

of the relative fixity of social roles and relations, though this fixity can be changed or even broken down.

I begin with the famous scene from *Vanity Fair*, which I think needs no defence or apology, only a fuller and closer recognition of its scope and depth in analysis and drama. Thackeray himself drew attention to one detail in Chapter 53 when he told James Hannay: 'When I wrote the sentence ['She admired her husband, strong, brave, and victorious.'], I slapped my fist on the table and said "that is a touch of genius".'[2]

It is precisely here that Thackeray's power seems most deserving of close scrutiny. There is indeed a sense of moral relief in the spectacle of Rawdon's action, and it involves a pleasure in seeing a favourite but degraded character expand, both morally and psychically. Rawdon has long had our approval, for his lovingness, his generosity, his fatherly tenderness, his innocence and his clumsiness. His rakish past, never very clear, has long sunk into a convenient haze, apart from his gambling, and here Becky's manipulation has carried responsibility and blame. In a novel where ascendancy in the pecking order carries such opprobrium – it testifies to the corruption of wit, intelligence, art, and the energies of greed, ambition and social aggression – there is the honourable degree of failure, shared by Rawdon, Briggs, Dobbin and other good innocents. But Thackeray allows us to have our cake and eat it in this reversal of the pecking order, this defeat of Becky and Lord Steyne, this triumph of a virtue sufficiently unideal, unheroic and mixed to attract free approval.

It is a triumph of Thackeray's moral satire that Rawdon's innocence and stupidity should be given this victory. It is a triumph of his psychological insight that the reader's approval should be shared by Becky, sufficiently a woman of her time to enjoy the virile display, even in her husband, and no less for

---

Chapter 53 (*Novels of the Eighteen-Forties*, Oxford: Oxford University Press, 1954), and Geoffrey Tillotson, brilliantly responsive to details of ironic imagery, is also apparently drawn to find non-dramatic matter to admire in this extraordinary scene (*Thackeray the Novelist*, Cambridge: Cambridge University Press, 1954). G. Armour Craig, in a later essay, 'On the Style of *Vanity Fair*' (in *Thackeray: A Collection of Critical Essays,* ed. A. Welsh, Englewood Cliffs, N.J.: Prentice-Hall, 1968), continues the apologetic or compensatory habit, in his judgment that in this scene 'the collision . . . misses its main issue and prize'.

[2] *A Brief Memoir of the Late Mr Thackeray* (Edinburgh, 1864).

its startling unfamiliarity. Reader's surprise is linked to character's. All this, and more, is felt as a direct consequence of the single physical stroke of Rawdon's 'arrest' of Steyne. This comes after three paragraphs in which Rawdon has said nothing, while Becky and Steyne have screamed, smiled, attempted laughter, tried to grin, protested innocence, denied innocence and so on. Then Rawdon, 'springing out, seized him by the neckcloth, until Steyne, almost strangled, writhed and bent under his arm. "You lie, you dog!" said Rawdon, "You lie, you coward and villain!" ' Rawdon's very inarticulateness, his simple, conventional, military language, has now come into its own, in the face of the failure in wit and art of these two clever overreachers. The sudden spring, the seizing of the neckcloth, and the blows, have the further triumph of reversing Rawdon's own physical arrest and humiliation of the previous night.

However, this kind of release has considerable complexity. It has been prepared for in Rawdon's very slow realization of Becky's betrayal, in his reading of her silence and absence, and last, in the letter where she finally shows how she underestimates his powers of mind. Moreover, the reader suddenly grasps much that has hitherto lain in the background of the soldier's character. Thackeray often knows much more about his characters than he lets on, and both Rawdon and Major Pendennis are abruptly revealed as capable of bravery and various strengths which are perfectly in character with their history as seasoned campaigners. There was always more to Rawdon than the rake and gambler, after all: now his military history, the decency, affection, toughness, generosity and recent nostalgia for youth, all come fully into their own. The dramatic scene here acts as a node for the character. It reflects back on our experience, showing the past to be more consistent and more complex than we knew, while also drawing on its implications for clarity of comprehension now. Once we reflect, it is surprising and yet inevitable that Rawdon should be brave, strong and victorious. Once we reflect, we find that we have been, like Becky, undervaluing the powers of a rather unintelligent and boring man.

Thackeray's touch of genius here is subtle; it is also consistent, typical and absolutely central. Not only does it show up the limitations of Becky's intelligence and artifice, in a way that arrests and challenges our own easy approval and interest, but it

also defines her present losses. At the moment – the only moment
– of appreciation, she loses Rawdon. Thackeray, for all his
celebrated 'intrusiveness', does not say and does not need to say
a word about this irony and nemesis. We feel it, in the reversal
and the release. Thackeray's conception of drama is dramatic
in the way of George Eliot and Henry James, who first put the
action 'inside'. In the most memorable scenes of such dramatic
triumphs as *Middlemarch* and *The Portrait of a Lady,* what
we now admire is the outer envelope of physical scene and its
inner psychic contents. Thackeray's method can be panoramic, as
Lubbock says, but it can also switch from panorama to inner
action. His method can be generalized, narrative, provisional and
non-committal, as other critics have said, but it can sharpen and
harden into lucid particulars. Chapter 53 of *Vanity Fair* (and
other scenes like it) can stand comparison with the best of George
Eliot and Henry James. There is the famous discovery scene in
Middlemarch where Dorothea interrupts and misinterprets a
passage between Rosamond Vincy and Will Ladislaw. There is
the scene in *The Portrait of a Lady* where Isobel Archer finds
her husband, Gilbert Osmond, that sterile stickler for etiquette
and convention, seated while Madame Merle stands. There is
the scene in *Felix Holt* where Harold Transome is suddenly told
that Jermyn is his father, in a brutal act of revelation before a
telltale mirror that insists on the resemblance. There is the scene
in *The Wings of the Dove* where Susan Shepherd Stringham
rushes in from the rain to tell Densher that Milly has turned
her face to the wall. In all these scenes, in varying degrees, outer
shock and inner action are matched. The matching is sometimes
conventional and straightforward as when the faces in the
mirror and the disturbance in the minds reflect and reinforce
each other's tumult. It is sometimes, as so often in James, presented through a contrast between outward nuance and inner
revelation. Isobel Archer reads the significance of the seated
man and the standing woman, revealing in the act of interpretation that she has by now been educated in the understanding
of such social nuances and stances and no longer believes as she
once did that human beings can be free of their outer coverings.
James places the shock further within the mind than Thackeray,
but his scenes exist, like Thackeray's, as discoveries and reversals
in the outer world, in rooms furnished with significant objects, in

people clothed purposefully, their properties, movements and gestures saturated with social and psychological meaning. And in Thackeray, granted a heavier emphasis on the outer than the inner action, there is the same sense that the vital discovery is both social and psychological. It is this double emphasis which gives his discovery scenes that very sense of free enactment whose absence Lubbock laments when he observes that Thackeray had given his men and women 'life and vigour enough for much more independence than they ever enjoyed'. This sense of the characters' independence is good testimony to the dramatic life of a novel, but I believe it applies to Thackeray's people as well as to George Eliot's and Henry James's.

In *Felix Holt* we register Harold Transome's sick shock of recognition as he sees his father's reflection aggressively forced upon him in a public place, eloquent of implications for his career, his sense of honour and his filial relations, and we are startled by the event in the outer world as a *coup de théâtre*, and also as a social act of considerable significance. We are also directed towards the psychological impact. Our surprise is a surprise about people, for the social act is one created and responded to by people. We learn to read character more sensitively, and see through a new emotional and moral experience the complexity and nature of the actors. Thackeray's Chapter 53 gives us a similar displacement and enlargement of social and psychological experience. We see Becky at a loss, not indeed for the first time, but more crucially than before. Then we see her sense of loss and guilt overcome by a feeling of admiration. We see in her resilient and instinctive acknowledgement of Rawdon's strength that brain and art are not the only means to mastery. We also see Steyne at a loss, uncontrolled and afraid, power, wit and irony falling to pieces. We see Rawdon in the ascendant, and not just because he is strong and brave but because the other two are put down morally, hence his commands and Becky's compliance. We also see the strange, sad blend of loss and gain, for Becky and Rawdon, in the terrible discovery. With all this goes that sense of the fascination of people, of their marvellous capacity to surprise and shock, which can accompany or even override profound or shattering crises. Thackeray is a brilliant analyst of ennui, and Becky's losses and punishments are in part defined in terms of ennui and boredom. In this scene, however, and for the first time, she is not bored by her husband. Her admiration for his victorious virility is a conventional sexual and social reaction, and it is on the cards that Thackeray was aware of this. Some of his critics have sentimentalized Becky,[3] but he himself kept a sure grasp of her own conventional little character. Hence her Royalism, and the way it displays itself. She is a climber, not a radical, and her moments of social criticism are merely sporadic.

Thackeray is pointing what he always appears to enjoy showing, a shift in the social and moral hierarchy. Becky is down, Steyne is down, Rawdon is up. Rawdon is in the ascendant in spite of his misery, and in spite of the conventional humiliation of the cuckold's position, which he challenges and overcomes. He is exposing the precariousness of social and intellectual gain, the shiftingness and shiftiness of the mobility and hierarchy of *Vanity Fair*, which in its class gains and its economic gains is fast-moving and chancy, very like a fairground, and very like England at the beginning of the century. But he is also revealing the chanciness of intelligence and wit, which have gained Becky so much hitherto. Some of Thackeray's most interesting revelations about Becky are her limitations, her inefficiencies and her failures, though it must be said that her capacity to put up with failure, to adapt and survive, is of course also an important part of the complex portraiture. Here Becky's discovery of her limitations, and her recognition of unfamiliar powers in another person, form part of a larger pattern of discovery in the novel. Amelia and Dobbin also have to learn the complexity of people by discovering limitation : Amelia has to recognize the limitations of her dead husband, Dobbin the limitations of Amelia herself; their personal revelation scene, where Dobbin tells Amelia that she is not worthy of his love, is another quieter and more inward-looking instance of Thackeray's concern with displacement and reversal.

Thackeray can lean as heavily as he likes on the externals – the dress, jewels, clothes, furniture, lights, movement – because at the centre of all the brilliant outer scene is his absolute confidence about people's feeling and thinking life. All the same, it would be shallow not to recognize his mastery of the social

---

[3] Elizabeth Jenkins, for instance, remarking strangely that Becky never deceives herself, in the introduction to the Everyman edition.

envelope. Becky has staged this scene, has arranged the lights, dressed the part, smothered herself with jewels, got rid of servants and husband, all the unwanted characters, like the clever producer and actress that she is, and the point can scarcely be missed when we recollect that the previous big scene showed the charades at Gaunt House, or that the intervening Chapter 52 showed the squalor of the sponging-house. The objects are aggressively present in social significance, both as unwholesome prizes, 'her own were all covered with serpents, and rings, and baubles', and as spoils of war : 'She began, trembling, pulling the jewels from her arms, and the rings from her shaking fingers, and held them all in a heap, quivering and looking up at him. "Throw them down," he said.' The objects remain significant to the end, after Rawdon's investigation of her desk, after her sense that she is left, dishevelled, 'dresses and feathers, scarfs and trinkets, a heap of tumbled vanities lying in a wreck', right up to the last enigmatic detail (not explained and complete until the next chapter) of the maid gathering up the trinkets from the floor. People are related to the objects, presents, trophies, spoils, ornaments, sleights, deceits, vanities, and Thackeray has his eye on the envelope, on the object, room, house. He is the kind of social novelist who knows the price and the value of everything. But he knows more than this. In the next chapter of *Vanity Fair*, in another scene of social reversal, the servants and rightful owners take possession of the drawing-room, the maraschino, the cream-dish, the little gilt glass and the beautiful chintz sofa. But Thackeray's marvellous eye for the social scene must not blind us to his interest in the mind and the feelings. The servants take over the spoils desperately, wretchedly and fearfully. His power as a novelist shifts our interest rapidly from the objects to the human response of Becky and her not very revolutionary victims. At his best, in these first major novels, it is a shift from outer to inner life which provides tension and elucidation. Thackeray strikes one as a Jamesian novelist in the complete sense of the term; he has the kind of mind on which nothing is lost – brooch, ring, banknote, painted face, emotional and intellectual activity.

In Chapters 53 and 54 the characters are all shocked, and the reader is too, as always in Thackeray at his best. (It is one of the great losses in *The Newcomes* that shocks and surprises come singly, slightly and almost predictably, as, for instance, in the revelation of Clive's marriage or the lost will, or Rosey's death.) But in Chapter 54 the reader may not only share Becky's earlier sense of Rawdon's limitation, but may well also have trouble with Thackeray's rendering of the 'problem' of technical adultery. I remember seeing a production of Pirandello's *As You Desire Me*, after which the audience went off still asking the question, *Was* it her, then? – a question which it had been the play's purpose to annihilate. I feel a similar sense of frustration and understanding when critics[4] continue to show interest in the answer Thackeray refused to give, to his question, 'What *had* happened? Was she guilty or not?' Thackeray has several good reasons for not answering, and for suggesting that this question and that of Becky's truthfulness on this one point are quite irrelevant. It is meaningless in the case of such large and proven corruption. We have been observing her lies for fifty chapters by now, and Thackeray is interested in truth and lies rather than in chastity, fidelity and adultery. Once again, his moral sense seems ahead of its time, and judging from much critical discussion, in some ways ahead of ours. Rawdon says, 'If she's not guilty, she's as bad as guilty', a remark which some critics have, most oddly, found shocking. G. Armour Craig,[5] for instance, observes the 'viciousness' of Rawdon's comment and concludes that the avoidance of an answer is a necessary but deplorable evasion on Thackeray's part. I conclude, rather, that it is grounded on a larger and more profound sense of value than that of sexual ethics. Thackeray is pointing to Becky's manipulation and betrayal of Rawdon, to the mean self-interest partly grasped in Rawdon's 'I always shared with you'. The reader has seen her meanness and treachery extend far beyond the secret hoarding to her pretence, to Lord Steyne, that Rawdon forced her to extort money. Hence the full irony of Steyne's reference to Rawdon as a 'bully'. The reader is in a better position to appreciate Steyne's misconception and the accuracy of Rawdon's 'as good as guilty' – Becky has manipulated not only Rawdon but his reputation, and in ways which make the

---

4 See, for example, G. Armour Craig in the article already cited (n. 1 above), and Leslie M. Thompson, 'Vanity Fair and the Johnsonian Tradition of Fiction', *The New Rambler*, C. VII (June 1969), 45-9.

5 Op. cit.

question of her actual adultery appear thinly technical. Disloyalty, deceit and the destruction of reputation, Thackeray is saying, are worse than adultery. Critics who fail to see this are perilously close to Becky, who is also unable to appreciate the finer points of morality, even if she is telling the truth when she says 'I am innocent'. It is Rawdon who is intuitively right about the moral position, and seeing his superior moral intelligence is another pleasure in our experience of enlightenment. Rawdon is shown as having an emotional and moral range that we had not appreciated, and the step forward in our understanding is both a realistic enhancing of character, and a process in the moral dynamics of the novel. What I have spoken of as the uncomfortable appraisal of what we had in common with Becky is entirely typical of Thackeray's art. He wants to make the reader uncomfortable, and succeeds.

A generalized sense that morality is more complex than we had thought comes through the particularity of learning that these people are less simple than we thought. In this process, the reading of a novel is not all that different from the intelligent experience of life. In *Vanity Fair*, the process partly depends on flexible and agile movement of satire. We look directly and critically at simplifications of judgment. Becky has seen Rawdon as a caricature, manageable, stupid, compliant, and disposed of him as such. She finds that he is rather different. But note how far Thackeray is from producing heroic surprises. It is true that we see that Rawdon's energy and honour are admirably alive, but if we start to admire him too fervently, we shall almost certainly be further disconcerted when he accepts the governorship. No heroics here, but a tough sense of revenge and survival. Likewise, in the scene where Rawdon asks Pitt to look after his child, Thackeray allows us in a certain fashion to enjoy the feeling of brotherly love and loyalty, especially refreshing after the exhibition of extreme cynicism and betrayal. But only after a fashion. Pitt first reveals his anxiety about money, and only when that priority is settled does he feel free to engage in a sincere enough show of brotherly feeling. Thackeray does not suggest that there is no such thing as disinterestedness, but he does say that disinterestedness is easier in certain circumstances than in others. As soon as Rawdon says 'It's not money I want', Pitt is able to show 'genuine alarm', 'commiseration', 'cordiality',

and to show himself as 'much affected'. Thackeray's treatment
of discovery is dependent on such a strong grasp of the complexity of the human passions and mind, on his refusal to create
caricature, except for his most shadowy nonce characters. And
although the characters whose complexity we most discern and
enjoy are the major ones, Becky, Amelia, Dobbin and George,
even lesser characters like Pitt and Lady Jane reflect the same
deep insight.

It is not only the reader who enjoys the human show. Becky,
most remarkably, also enjoys and appreciates the surprises of
human nature, and on many occasions Thackeray manages to
draw with one stroke her appreciation of her own complexity
and that of nature. Like Pitt, she is also hardly ever capable of
disinterestedness. It is, for instance, noticeable that her enjoyment
of Rawdon's virility is quickly followed by her feeling that she
may still be able to keep something back from him.[6] Often what
she appreciates is bound up with her own self-love, as when she
enjoys her technical defeat at the hands of the gentle and compliant Lady Jane (another reversal in the social and psychic
order) because she realizes that Jane's attack is a jealous one and
therefore very flattering. But she is not fully sensitive to Lady
Jane's moral disgust, which proceeds not only from jealousy but
from her maternal disapproval of Becky's hypocrisy and harsh-
ness about little Rawdon. As ever, Thackeray is immensely
subtle. Becky is not good at appreciating real disinterestedness
and does not read Jane with total accuracy. The same subtlety
emerges in the scene towards the end when Becky magnani-
mously (but not wholly unindulgently) produces the letter George
hid in her bouquet long ago, and uses it in order to persuade Amelia to give up the false idol and send for Dobbin. When
Amelia adds a further surprise to the scene by admitting that
she has already done this, Becky enjoys the disclosure with her
usual appreciative gusto : 'Becky screamed with laughter – " *Un
biglietto*," she sang out with Rosina, *"eccolo qua!"* – the whole
house echoed with her shrill singing.' Her perception of Amelia's
unexpected and untypical action modulates cleverly from the
earlier touch – 'soothed and kissed her – a rare mark of
sympathy with Mrs Becky' – so that we are back in the

---

[6] In this case, money and knowledge.

rather crude, shrill, coarser world of the operatic exclamation. Becky's appreciation exists, but Thackeray loses no opportunity of pointing out its bluntness. He also refuses to make her too strong an agent of good; Amelia herself brings Dobbin back, Becky is permitted the gesture but not the responsibility. And Becky, like the reader, has underestimated Amelia's powers of action and feeling. But the impression of Becky's resilience and limited but vivacious sensibility goes on right to the end of the novel. She really does appreciate Dobbin. She takes a fair measure of Amelia's strength and weakness. She hankers (almost pathetically) after the style and wit of Lord Steyne, for an instant stupidly supposing that she may still have some power over him. In all these instances, Becky is shown as demonstrating her mind and feelings. Though she is almost exclusively confined to histrionic display, she can occasionally behave naturally. She can also behave fairly well when there is nothing at stake. She can be kind, understanding, and appreciative of integrity and depth. It is a point that Jane Austen makes in creating her version of corrupt wit, art and sexual charm in Mary Crawford. Mary, like Becky, can act decently and sympathetically to Fanny, for instance, when the action and the feeling are inexpensive. Jane Austen and Thackeray both knew and showed that the point about moral appreciation and sympathy is not that wicked people are incapable of such acts of love, but that they seldom feel free to perform them. The psychology of moral action and the realistic creation of character are enriched by Thackeray's perception and his dramatic enactment of it.

In such instances, then, Thackeray puts the reader through a process of change and recognition. Not only does he refuse to let us enjoy mind and wit overmuch, but he also refuses to let us indulge too zealously and reverently in moral admiration. Unlike Henry James, he never overrates brains: he endowed Dobbin with 'fairly good brains', and did call him Dobbin. Unlike George Eliot, he never overrates intense feeling either; he knows that the heart can be stupid too (like Amelia's and Dobbin's), and he does not feel that awe, veneration or worship should lie beyond the reach of censure. His criticism of strong feeling is probably one of the chief reasons why he is so uncomfortable a novelist, depriving us of intellectual flattery, moral superiority and emotional indulgence all at once.

B

There are of course compensations. If our feelings at times appear to expand into unwonted respect or sympathy for Becky or Lord Steyne, only to be firmly constricted and put in their proper place, so there are some characters, like Rawdon, for whom our enlarged respect may be tempered and qualified but survives as a firm gain. This sense of expanded knowledge and respect is fairly rare, but we experience it more in *Vanity Fair* than in any other novel. In Dobbin's case we also see another reversal – the worm turning – but we have absolutely no need to learn anything new about his capacity for devotion, honour or love. What we discover about him is that like Rawdon he is capable of a critical discrimination we had not known about; there is not only the pleasure of having him criticize Amelia, but the additional delight in having him step out of the role of self-effacing hanger-on, spoony and Dobbin. It may be argued – though once more Thackeray leaves us to observe it for ourselves – that Amelia is not unlike Becky in learning to appreciate the quality of a man at the moment of loss. Becky and Amelia are both made to realize that there is nothing like deprivation to make us appreciate what we lose. Moreover, they are both made to feel the attraction of energy and attack. Amelia too sees the man she has underrated turn on her, change roles, attack vigorously and gain a victory :

'Have I not learned in that time to read all your feelings, and look into your thoughts? I know what your heart is capable of : it can cling faithfully to a recollection, and cherish a fancy; but it can't feel such an attachment as mine deserves to mate with, and such as I would have won from a woman more generous than you. No, you are not worthy of the love which I have devoted to you. I knew all along that the prize I had set my life on was not worth the winning; that I was a fool, with fond fancies, too, bartering away my all of truth and ardour against your little feeble remnant of love. I will bargain no more : I withdraw. I find no fault with you. You are very good-natured, and have done your best; but you couldn't – you couldn't reach up to the height of the attachment which I bore you, and which a loftier soul than yours might have been proud to share. Good-bye, Amelia ! I have watched your struggle. Let it end. We are both weary of it.'

Amelia stood scared and silent as William thus suddenly broke

the chain by which she held him, and declared his independence
and superiority. He had placed himself at her feet so long that
the poor little woman had been accustomed to trample upon him.
She didn't wish to marry him, but she wished to keep him. She
wished to give him nothing, but that he should give her all. It is
a bargain not unfrequently levied in love. (Chap. 66)

Once more, Thackeray does not show all his hand. In the
big scene in Chapter 53 there are two important things held back;
we do not gather immediately the full implications of the maid
picking up the trinkets, and the last paragraph leaves a little
serial trail from one chapter to another, adding in delayed effect
a small but sharp irony. We also do not know yet the answer
(or non-answer) to the question about Becky's innocence. The
time-lag here in Chapter 67 also involves something small and
something large. Becky intends to plot for Dobbin, and the
reader is allowed to see her full and disinterested appreciation
of his nobility without yet being shown Thackeray's refusal to let
her be a good agent. More important, we are shown and told
a little about Amelia's surprise, discomfiture and selfishness, but
Thackeray leaves the narrative of her feelings incomplete. What
the reader is left with is not only a very functional loose end or
two, valuable in the plotting, and permitting future tension,
surprise and climax, but a surprise in character. Here we see
Thackeray's tremendous skill in handling a dynamic plot and in
centring attention on the psychic point. Dobbin has changed, is
Dobbin no longer, and Amelia and Becky both act as sensitive
registers of that change. But the change itself registers impressions
of Amelia and Becky: Dobbin turns because Amelia has shown
herself intolerably ungrateful and selfish, and his fine disgust, as
he throws away Becky's note, is the final touch in this record of
his honourable energy.

Once changed, like Rawdon, he remains a finer, larger and
sadder character, returning to Amelia, but reserving judgment
and heart. The last we see of him is the brilliantly true and
hard glimpse at the very end, when we are taking a choric
farewell of the characters at a Fancy Fair. At this point we may
not be expecting either another development or a reminder of
that earlier enlargement. Dobbin, Emmy and their children see
and shrink from Becky. Thackeray has on a previous page

laconically defined Dobbin's reluctance to leave home in this way: 'The Colonel quitted home with reluctance (for he was deeply immersed in his "History of the Punjaub" which still occupies him, and much alarmed about his little daughter, whom he idolises, and who was just recovering from the chicken-pox).' His wife is here conspicuous by her absence, but in case absence is not quite conspicuous enough, the author makes the point more clearly in his final paragraphs:

. . . the Colonel seizing up his little Janey, of whom he is fonder than of anything in the world – fonder even than of his 'History of the Punjaub'.

'Fonder than he is of me,' Emmy thinks, with a sigh. But he never said a word to Amelia that was not kind and gentle; or thought of a want of hers that he did not try to gratify.

This kind of refusal to maintain worship, only sustained, I believe, in *Vanity Fair* and *Esmond,* perhaps explains why some readers consider Thackeray cynical or feel that his is the kind of toughness that is very close to cynicism. He is not cynical: there is a refreshing, exhilarating and even optimistic sense that Rawdon and Dobbin are more sensitive, intelligent and energetic than we supposed, and that virtue need not be self-effacing, docile or wormlike. But there is no doubt that this admission and reversal, especially in Dobbin's case, is proffered as an example of human vanity, neither Dobbin nor Amelia discovering what they expected in attaining what they desired. One might say that the only character who is never saddened by this particular form of vanity is Becky, who lacks the necessary faith and love to encounter loss. As we admire her toughness and resilience, as Thackeray cunningly tempts us to do, we should recognize that the faithless and heartless, the entirely corrupt, lacking any ideal, cannot suffer from lost desire.

This expansion and displacement is, then, the original and complex mode of proceeding in *Vanity Fair*. Scenically and psychologically, Thackeray continued to use the same process in subsequent novels, but it is entirely missing in *Philip* and even in *The Newcomes,*[7] where its absence is one of the flaws in

[7] I am not concerned with *Catherine, Barry Lyndon* and other novels and stories where the action is not psychological.

Thackeray's last major novel. The method is particularly appropriate to *Vanity Fair*, showing as it does a process of loss and frustration, chiefly for Becky, but for other characters as well; it also permits Thackeray at once to chronicle loss and a certain sad growth of wisdom, as opposed to wit, in Rawdon and Dobbin. But besides dramatizing vanity and frustration, it expresses a psychological interest which is always developed in the drama of social environment.

The great reversal scene in *Pendennis* involves Major Pendennis, a very important character, with whom the novel begins and ends; he is the prime agent in the corruption of Pendennis, the hero, and represents all things worldly – social and military success, a lightly stressed dissoluteness, fogydom, non-attachment, and even, at times, a kind of humiliating lackeydom in his relation to great men, particularly Lord Steyne who, like so many other characters, creates continuity between *Vanity Fair* and *Pendennis*. Great fleas have lesser fleas – and Morgan, Pendennis's man, is the gentleman's gentleman, or the lackey's lackey. The first big scene I have in mind involves the staggering social and personal reversal of roles in Morgan's rise against the Major, in Chapter 67, 'In Which the Major Is Bidden to Stand and Deliver'. Chapter 67 begins slowly. We see Morgan laying his plans and biding his time 'with silent, obsequious fidelity', and we hear about the Major's rather bad autumn, his reputation being 'somewhat on the wane', and many a London door now closed that had been open. The Major is being forced into an awareness 'that he was no longer of the present age and . . . that the young men laughed at him', and comes back from a not very good holiday to a not very welcoming London. Thackeray presents the melancholy, the loneliness, the desolation of the selfish old man :

> Old Pendennis had no special labours or bills to encounter on the morrow, as he had no affection at home to soothe him. He had always money in his desk sufficient for his wants; and being by nature and habit tolerably indifferent to the wants of other people, these latter were not likely to disturb him. But a gentleman may be out of temper though he does not owe a shilling : and though he may be ever so selfish, he must

occasionally feel dispirited and lonely. He had had two or three twinges of gout in the country-house where he had been staying : the birds were wild and shy, and the walking over the ploughed fields had fatigued him deucedly : the young men had laughed at him, and he had been peevish at table once or twice : he had not been able to get his whist of an evening : and, in fine, was glad to come away. In all his dealings with Morgan, his valet, he had been exceedingly sulky and discontented. He had sworn at him and abused him for many days past. He had scalded his mouth with bad soup at Swindon. He had left his umbrella in the railroad carriage : at which piece of forgetfulness he was in such a rage, that he cursed Morgan more freely than ever. Both the chimneys smoked furiously in his lodgings; and when he caused the windows to be flung open, he swore so acrimoniously, that Morgan was inclined to fling him out of window, too, through that opened casement. The valet swore after his master, as Pendennis went down the street on his way to the club.

Bays's was not at all pleasant. The house had been new painted, and smelt of varnish and turpentine, and a large streak of white paint inflicted itself on the back of the old boy's fur-collared surtout. The dinner was not good : and the three most odious men in all London – old Hawkshaw, whose cough and accompaniments are fit to make any man uncomfortable; old Colonel Gripley, who seizes on all the newspapers; and that irreclaimable old bore Jawkins, who would come and dine at the next table to Pendennis, and describe to him every inn-bill which he had paid in his foreign tour; each and all of these disagreeable personages and incidents had contributed to make Major Pendennis miserable; and the club waiter trod on his toe as he brought him his coffee. Never alone appear the Immortals. The Furies always hunt in company : they pursued Pendennis from home to the club and from the club home. (Chap. 67)

Thackeray also describes Mrs Brixham, Morgan's parasite or slave, and shows Morgan drinking while he is served by her; Morgan is then reprimanded by the Major and sworn at for delay, clumsiness and drunkenness while he takes off the Major's boots. The Major inflamed by temper, and Morgan inflamed by brandy, the great quarrel begins :

'I'm drunk, am I? I'm a beast, am I? I'm d—d, am I? you infernal old miscreant. Shall I wring your old head off, and drownd yer in that pail of water? Do you think I'm a-goin' to

bear your confounded old harrogance, you old Wigsby! Chatter
your old hivories at me, do you, you grinning old baboon? Come
on, if you are a man, and can stand to a man. Ha! you coward,
knives, knives!'

'If you advance a step, I'll send it into you,' said the major,
seizing up a knife that was on the table near him. 'Go downstairs,
you drunken brute, and leave the house; send for your book and
your wages in the morning, and never let me see your insolent
face again. This d—d impertinence of yours has been growing
for some months past. You have been growing too rich. You are
not fit for service. Get out of it, and out of the house.'

'And where would you wish me to go, pray, out of the 'ouse?'
asked the man, 'and won't it be equal convenient to-morrow
mornin'? – tootyfay mame shose, sivvaplay, munseer?'

'Silence, you beast, and go!' cried out the major.

Morgan began to laugh, with rather a sinister laugh. 'Look yere,
Pendennis,' he said, seating himself; 'since I've been in this room
you've called me a beast, brute, dog : and d—d me, haven't you?
How do you suppose one man likes that sort of talk from another?
How many years have I waited on you, and how many damns
and cusses have you given me, along with my wages? Do you think
a man's a dog, that you can talk to him in this way? If I choose to
drink a little why shouldn't I? I've seen many a gentleman drunk
formly, and peraps have the 'abit from them. I ain't a-goin' to
leave this house, old feller, and shall I tell you why? The house is
my house; every stick of furnitur' in it is mine, excep' *your* old
traps, and your shower-bath, and your wig-box. I've bought the
place, I tell you, with my own industry and perseverance. I can
show a hundred pound, where you can show a fifty, or your
damned supersellious nephew either. I've served you honourable,
done everythink for you these dozen years, and I'm a dog, am
I? I'm a beast, am I? That's the language for gentlemen, not for
our rank. But I'll bear it no more. I throw up your service :
I'm tired on it; I've combed your old wig and buckled your old
girths and waistbands long enough, I tell you. Don't look savage
at me. I'm sitting in my own chair, in my own room, a-telling
the truth to you. I'll be your beast, and your brute, and your
dog, no more, Major Pendennis 'Alf Pay.' (Ibid.)

At this point the psychological surprises begin, coming as
usual from a reciprocal response, the Major's temper cooling
because Morgan's speech interests him. 'He rather respected his
adversary, and his courage in facing him, as of old days, in the

MR. MORGAN AT HIS EASE

fencing-room, he would have admired the opponent who hit him.'
Throughout the scene, the emphasis is on two things: on the
sheer interest of the reversal and the quarrel to the bored old man;
and also on the vivid revival of earlier days, of fighting, fencing
and 'affairs'. The Major dismisses the man, calmly and with
great dignity, and then muses by the fireside, his testiness gone,
feeling the inconvenience of having to lose his servant and leave
his lodgings, but most of all feeling the excitement of what has
happened. Then Mrs Brixham comes in to tell her troubles, and
just as the 'superior excitement' drives away the 'testiness', so
the poor lady's fear of Morgan makes him forget his troubles in
his 'compassion' for her. The chapter ends with a cool reflection
on Morgan's threat to bring him to his knees: 'Me on my
knees? . . . Who ever saw me on my knees? What the devil does
the fellow know? Gad, I've not had an affair these twenty years.
I defy him.' Excited and amused, 'the old campaigner turned
round and slept pretty sound'.

This big scene is spread over the next chapter too, and
Chapter 68 begins with a polite encounter as Morgan opens
the shutters and does the usual offices, enraged by the Major's
politeness. After the Major has packed, with the aid of the
substitute servant thoughtfully provided by Morgan, the second
encounter takes place. Morgan feels that their old master-servant
relationship is quite at an end, and the time ripe for revelation
and blackmail: 'I know of a marriage as is no marriage – of a
honourable baronet as is no more married than I am. . . .' In
other words, the biter is bit, the blackmailer blackmailed. But
when Morgan demands the cheque, the Major picks up the
'little double-barrelled pistol, which had belonged to Pendennis's
old patron, the Indian commander-in-chief, and which had
accompanied him in many a campaign', and we are back in
the old relationship of authority and power, though with a
difference.

There follows the encounter with the policeman, in which the
Major gambles on Morgan's being a thief, and then stops short
as he reflects (self-interestedly) that the man might be dangerous,
and (disinterestedly) that he may be able to make terms for Mrs
Brixham. He dictates the letter to Morgan, makes him return
Mrs Brixham's note of hand, gets the policeman to witness the
paper, organizes the packing and the cab, and departs in

triumph : '. . . the stout old boy could afford not to be frightened at Mr Morgan, and flung him a look of great contempt and humour as he strutted away with his cane'.

He remains the 'old boy', and remains slightly ridiculous, with strut and cane and wig, but Thackeray has suggested the reality of that military glory which seemed so shadowy, and we believe in the Major as a man of courage, resource and authority.

Thackeray does not create a complete reversal : the Major has already been characterized as a military figure, as having dignity and resourcefulness, and has never been without humour and some compassion. But the scene demonstrates each quality with vigour. Like Rawdon, his soldiering has been done off-stage, but the retrospect endorses and motivates the present scene, which has itself a solid background and strength. Thackeray had conceived the Major in the round; his was a real courage and capacity, and the Major will never appear ridiculous, stereotyped or boring again. Other things also fall into place : Steyne respected him, he was not just a figure of fun, fogy, lackey, old rake. Nor does Thackeray sentimentalize here any more than he did with Rawdon : the Major is the old lady's preserver, but we see him ponder the exact sum he can give her, ten pounds or twenty, just as we see him consider the expediency of letting the policeman arrest Morgan for theft, then consider the dangers and difficulties. His pity is noted, qualified, then his coolness, his quick temper, his resentment, his sense of expediency. The calculations and the passions go together, in brilliant Thackerayan fashion, strong and touching. Morgan and the Major emerge from the scene enlarged, different, in a different relation to each other, in which the moral ironies are rich, though Thackeray does not choose to remark on them explicitly. Another novelist might have dwelt on the similarity of the moral position of the two blackmailers, but Thackeray is more interested in the shifts of the social and personal relation. The tension, contrast and mobility of the scene have little to do with strong moral climax and everything to do with a sense of personal and social life. The author does not draw our attention to the play of character, but lets it show itself in the drama and in the analysis of mind, feeling and relationship.

However, the drama does not end here. Thackeray's big scenes have their localized dramatic structure, with beginning, middle, end, tension and climax. And they have the social and psychological drama, also localized, though proving on inspection to be linked causally with the past and future. But the scene between Morgan and the Major is not a turning-point in the action, though it may look like one for a little while. Towards the end of the scene, the Major, departing in triumph, 'strutted away with his cane'. He is seen by his author respectfully and comically. The comic element is perhaps sinister, since the triumph, though real in personal professional terms, is short-lived and deceptive.

There is a gap of two line-spaces and then Morgan is slowly put once more in the ascendant. Arthur Pendennis, involved unknowingly in his uncle's shady scheme and elegant blackmail, comes along to receive Morgan's information, and as a result, to reject the Major's worldly conformity and compromise, in money, political career and marriage, that the secret schemes represent. Once more, Thackeray has a sense of the drama and rebuking irony of the shift in social role as Arthur speaks in a peremptory and 'insolent and good-natured way' to the servant : 'Do you want my uncle to take you back?' Morgan is grave and respectful, but tempering the deference – 'bowing, but not touching the elegant cap which he wore' and says, 'I want no such thing; I'd see him —.' He softly asks Arthur to walk 'into my house' and Arthur innocently and arrogantly does so, thinking, 'I suppose the fellow wants me to patronise him.' The very last sentence refuses to dramatize, resting drily on previous knowledge : 'A card was already in the front windows, proclaiming that apartments were to be let, and having introduced Mr Pendennis into the dining-room, and offered him a chair, Mr Morgan took one himself, and proceeded to convey some information to him, with which the reader has already had cognizance.'

All the drama indeed goes underground, because the next Chapter, 69, 'In Which Pendennis Counts His Eggs', is craftily placed so as to show precisely the dangers of premature egg-counting, since it deals with a conversation between Pen and Warrington earlier on the same day. It curves back in time and ends by bringing us to the point where Arthur goes off to see the Major, having been sent off by Lady Rockminster, who takes the reader's earlier view of the Major – 'You will not bring him to dinner – no – his old stories are intolerable'. Chapter 70 begins with Pen's return, in order to relate Morgan's disclosures to

Warrington and Laura. The title of this chapter is a popular
quotation from Horace, to be truly endorsed, 'Fiat Justitia', and
here the novel reaches its moral crisis : 'I have sinned, but, Heaven
help me, I will sin no more.' Arthur's words are melodramatic,
perhaps, but they do mark a crisis in a complex social and moral
theatre. Here the Major is really brought low. Now he does go on
his decrepit old knees, and prays, blasphemously and corruptly, in
the name of God, family honour, pride, affection and greed, that
Arthur should not throw away rank and money : 'It's the making
of you. You're sure to get on. You'll be a baronet; it's three
thousand a year : dammy, on my knees, there, I beg of you,
don't do this.'

This reversal is not only one of power and triumph, but stresses
age and impotence : 'And the old man actually sank down on
his knees, and seizing one of Arthur's hands, looked up piteously
at him. It was cruel to remark the shaking hands, the wrinkled
and quivering face, the old eyes weeping and winking, the
broken voice.' He loses, and ends with an extraordinary speech
compounded of pathos, worldly blasphemy, twisted quotation,
and unobtrusive ironies :

> 'I have done my best, and said my say; and I'm a dev'lish
> old fellow. And – and – it don't matter. And – and – Shakespeare
> was right – and Cardinal Wolsey – begad "and had I but served
> my God as I've served you" – yes, on my knees, by Jove, to my
> own nephew – I mightn't have been – Good-night, sir; you
> needn't trouble yourself to call again.'
>
> Arthur took his hand, which the old man left to him; it was
> quite passive and clammy. He looked very much oldened; and it
> seemed as if the contest and defeat had quite broken him.
>
> On the next day he kept his bed, and refused to see his
> nephew. (Chap. 70)

Thackeray, then, renews surprise and reversal. Here he follows
full dramatic display with reserve, with enigmatic and ironic
withholding of information. We are never to see directly, only
to glimpse and infer, what Morgan and Pen said to each other
and how Pen replied. Thackeray produces a seesaw action, only
effectively surprising and animated in itself, and also testifying
to the mobility of power in his society. (Morgan later looks like
coming to a bad end, as he continues as blackmailer and spy,

but finishes as 'one of the most respectable men in the parish of St James's, and in the present political movement has pronounced himself like a man and a Briton', thus quietly but sharply contributing to Thackeray's analysis of conservatism and respectability.) In the scene between Pen and the Major there is the reversal of youth and age, pupil and mentor, and the much larger reversal and discovery of Pen's worldliness and corruption. The scene demonstrates Thackeray's sense of dramatic continuity and his psychological mixture : we do feel sorry for the decrepit old soldier, no longer dignified, resourceful, victorious, the sorrier for having seen him so recently in the ascendant. It also shows his quiet but concrete drama of social observation in the details of name and gesture. Morgan bows but does not touch his cap. His cap is elegant. Thackeray carefully calls him 'Morgan' when he is servant, or treated as servant, and 'Mr Morgan' when he is master and houseowner, or ironically but logically treated as such by the Major : 'Mr Morgan and I have arranged our little dispute.' The uses of title in Thackeray are as pointed as the forms of address in *Emma* or the modulations on 'thou' and 'you' in Marlowe's *Edward II* or Thomas Mann's *The Magic Mountain*, though very much less marked and explicit than in those works. Thackeray's quiet social observation (muted further, of course, by time) has a special sting.

Social details of address and etiquette are quiet but crucial in my last example, which comes from *Henry Esmond*. Like the earlier instances, it involves much more than social record, being a turning-point in relationships. Like the *Vanity Fair* discovery scene and the scene I have just discussed in *Pendennis*, it creates a moral crisis and a great change for the hero. But before I come to it, I want to say a word about the novel's many scenes of discovery. We may say, perhaps, that discovery rather than reversal is typical of *Esmond*. It is a novel which makes lavish use of discovery scenes, frequently in a covert and ironic way, since the complete truth, only glimpsed, hinted or revealed piecemeal, is cumulatively guessed by the reader as by Henry Esmond himself. The drama in which Rachel transfers her feelings from her 'Lord' to Esmond, the enacted recognition that Esmond's love for Rachel is more stable and rational (though less profound?) than his love for Beatrix, and the discovery that his love for Beatrix is transient, ignorant and doomed, are three main threads in the plot spun in this novel by the passions. The weaving of all three threads is incomplete until the end of the novel. One might say that the typical discovery scene in *Esmond* is a veiled one, like the scene of Rachel's apparent disturbance over Harry's contact with smallpox, the scene where she decides to use her legacy to send him to Cambridge, and the scene where she visits him in prison. In all these episodes there are two proffered readings; the innocent reading selects one discovery and fails to make the other, or selects one but casts doubt and uncertainty over its accuracy. There are some scenes that show their meaning more clearly; the famous instance in church where Rachel weeps with hysterical joy over the 'sheaves' is certainly a typical discovery scene in making a climax of action – reconciliation – coincide with a sense of emotional revelation.

Esmond is a novel about secrets, mysteries and illusions, and culminates in one splendid scene of discovery and reversal which ends the twin passions of Henry's political and personal life. It involves the social unmasking, the shift in roles and the reciprocal psychological discovery. It also resembles the other scenes I have discussed in having a typically Thackerayan enigmatic cunning. Although the Pretender is made to express his sorrow at losing Beatrix – the most beautiful woman in the world – we already know that he had not lost her, and we may guess that while Esmond is made to feel that the music and drama are ended, his happy marriage, prose though it may be, is yet to come. But the rest of the novel is not only presented in narrative summary (evasive or eloquent) but is handled reticently and indeed reverently. Chapter 13 of Book 3 is the last fully exposed dramatic close-up in the novel. Indeed, throughout, Thackeray's technique is to show Esmond's feeling for Rachel darkly, reticently, obliquely, his feeling for Beatrix openly, visibly, nakedly. The exposed and reticent manners carry with them some implications for the passions being treated: the feeling for his 'mistress', being both unexplored, partly unadmitted and unacknowledged, the feeling for Beatrix being obsessionally and recklessly revealed to the reader and to every character.

This scene reveals new emotional and psychological life in two

other characters, in the Pretender, and in Harry's cousin, Frank
Esmond, who rather clumsily but 'honourably' seconds Henry's
actions and responses. As in *Vanity Fair*, Thackeray is writing
a discovery scene in which the mere fact of sexual surrender is
made relatively unimportant. Esmond reflects that though they
may save Beatrix's 'person', they are too late to save her mind –
'had she not instigated the young Prince to come to her;
suborned servants, dismissed others, so that she might com-
municate with him? The treacherous heart within her had
surrendered, though the place was safe; and it was to win this
that he had given a life's struggle and devotion'. Esmond first
speaks to the Prince very formally, revealing his feelings in a
generalized irony – 'the Queen may be dead in spite of the
doctor' – and in an insistent harping on the titles of 'the Prince
of Wales' against 'King' and 'Majesty'. This stroke of rhetoric
makes itself apparent to the Prince himself, who is goaded by
the stress and irony and says so. Not only his style but his
behaviour is aggressive and rude, though in the negative form of
not helping the Prince 'to his coat'. After making it plain that
they have come 'to avenge, and not to compass, the dishonour
of our family', Esmond continues the social offensive by making
grim jokes about the Prince's rhymes, which he would not have
been playing with had he, in Esmond's words, 'been happy'.
Gradually the covert attacks and *double entendres* mount until
politeness and wit abruptly break down. The play and the
breakdown reveal a new seriousness in the Prince, whose weight-
iness has not been apparent at all till now, but comes out in his
sadness about the loss of the English Crown, Beatrix, and the
allegiance of 'such hearts' as Henry's and Frank's. He is revealed
in a new emotional range, showing fury, a sensitive response to
courtly insult, and a volatile movement from anger through
humiliation to generous admission, 'in his eager way', of the
losses. Even Esmond is 'extremely touched' by the offer to cross
swords. The Prince's lack of control – evident in his initial slow
understanding, then speedy response and reaction of fury, contrition, grief and affection – shows his familiar charm and
animation but in a fresh context. And Esmond's control, coldness, deep sense of loss, and continued feeling of respect and
appreciation, also keep old characteristics alive and extend them
in a new situation. The social reversal is inseparable from the

psychological: up to now, Esmond has not been able to show himself so completely and humanly to the Prince, nor has the Prince so exposed and offered his own humanity. The scene moves through a wide and surprising range, surprising the reader and surprising the characters, right up to the entry of Beatrix who hisses her hatred to Esmond at the moment when he reflects on the death of his passion for her. The dialogue at any one point may seem theatrical, but taking this mobile, complex scene as a whole, there is a counterbalancing stress on inner change.

The culmination is Esmond's recognition that they have all lost; he too, like the Prince, has lost his political adventure, his career, his stake and his love:

> But her keen words gave no wound to Mr Esmond; his heart was too hard. As he looked at her, he wondered that he could ever have loved her. His love of ten years was over; it fell down dead on the spot, at the Kensington Tavern, where Frank brought him the note out of Eikon Basilike. The Prince blushed and bowed low, as she gazed at him, and quitted the chamber. I have never seen her from that day. (Bk 3, Chap. 13)

The various forms available within the novel, the third-person 'Mr', 'Colonel', 'Esmond' or the first-person 'I', can indicate reserve and unreserve, and within a short space. The 'I' here indicates a personal feeling, of regret and finality, in contrast to the more controlled and cold rejections of 'no wound to Mr Esmond'. The 'Mr' is itself significant, eloquent of the end of a military career, since the only title Esmond has claimed, that of Colonel, is the one used throughout the scene with the Prince. The shifts of title are especially marked in this novel.

In this scene, too, social particularity is strong. The careful rituals of action – the burning of the title, the crossing of the swords, the refusal to help, reinforce the social implications of the chosen titles, whether 'Colonel', 'Mr', 'I', 'Frank', 'Castlewood', 'the Prince', 'the young Prince', 'his Majesty', 'the Prince of Wales' or 'the Marquis of Esmond'. Beside the local shifts, the careful and explicit choice of titles makes it plain that this is a novel about title, about bastardy, about claiming and essaying thrones, allegiance, fealty and legitimacy of several kinds. Beatrix, Frank, Esmond, Rachel and the Prince are all people engaged in social and political relations as well as in intimate passions, and Thackeray's marked social drama in this discovery scene makes his private and public themes very evident. The action is psychological and emotional, the reversals and changes within; but action and reversals are also social, even public. So he insists on the social time and place, on the social significance of language and manners, and, above all, on the social causes and effects of private life.

Moreover, the combination of private and public, in these big scenes, is always very explicit, the characters themselves shown as quite aware of their circumstances. Where social humiliation figures in Thackeray's novels, it is fully felt, as by Lord Steyne or the Prince, or significantly not felt, and rejected, as by Esmond, Major Pendennis and Rawdon. And the awareness is one of estate, in the fullest and oldest sense of that term, being a matter of class and of profession. It is notable that in three of Thackeray's reversal scenes, the military identity of character – in Rawdon, Major Pendennis and Colonel Esmond – is well to the fore, and goes against the class divisions, in at least two cases.

To sum up, these big scenes of reversal show a grasp of outer and inner action, and of the social circumstances of class, work, possessions, that relates the people, and to a large extent creates and defines actions and reactions. In these reversal scenes the characters' social identity is insisted on, either because it is related to a reserve of personal power that the scene draws on, or because it is under trial, in the scene's social reversal. Becky's price is clearly evidenced in the objects and finery of Chapter 53; Rawdon the soldier is needed, and acts; Steyne's magnificence, at bay, is brought out to be defeated. In *Pendennis*, mastery is challenged, then redefined in two scenes that show very plainly a whole hierarchy of command and servitude and compensatory bullying, as well as permitting a new definition, and therefore justification, for Major Pendennis's authority. In the *Esmond* scene, authority, allegiance and title are all revalued, passed through the fire and criticized, readjusted, and to some extent comprehended and admired. In these key scenes which achieve turning-points in the action, Thackeray employs the psychology of social class and relationships to rich effect.

CHAPTER TWO

Art and Nature

Thence passing forth, they shortly do arriue,
    Whereas the Bowre of *Blisse* was situate;
    A place pickt out by choice of best aliue,
    That natures worke by art can imitate:
    In which what euer in this worldly state
    Is sweet, and pleasing vnto liuing sense,
    Or that may dayntiest fantasie aggrate,
    Was poured forth with plentifull dispence,
And made there to abound with lauish affluence.

Goodly it was enclosed round about,
    Aswell their entred guestes to keepe within,
    As those vnruly beasts to hold without;
    Yet was the fence thereof but weake and thin;
    Nought feard their force, that fortilage to win,
    But wisedomes powre, and temperaunces might,
    By which the mightiest things efforced bin:
    And eke the gate was wrought of substaunce light,
Rather for pleasure, then for battery or fight.

The Faerie Queene, Bk 2, Can. 12

One of the major implications of the title and main image of *Vanity Fair* is the corruption of nature by greed, deceit and art. Thackeray approves of honesty, sincerity and spontaneity, and criticizes posing and artifice. The critical emphasis varies, falling on heartlessness or hypocrisy or exhibitionism or artful manipulation, and sometimes on all four simultaneously. Everyone knows that the chief performance in *Vanity Fair* is that given by 'the famous little Becky puppet', as Thackeray describes her in the preliminary address, 'Before the Curtain'. At the very beginning of her performance, in Chapter 1, 'Chiswick Mall', Thackeray does not show Becky's accomplishments as artist, actress and performer, but rather establishes the environment in which performance becomes necessary. He begins his novel with a critique of Becky's environment which certainly goes far to create and explain her histrionic ways: it shows a hierarchy of power, a pecking-order in which Becky is as yet only finding her way, and it very clearly reveals the incompatibility of success – defined as money and power – with nature, heart, sincerity or love. As yet, Becky is only a novice and learner, as befits a character who is on the brink of leaving school. Her performance has scarcely begun, but Thackeray's analysis of performance is already complex.

The school itself is one of those totally assimilated social symbols which exist in full and self-contained particularity in Thackeray's satiric world: schooling, learning, achievement, testimonials, teaching, finishing the course, are metaphors as well as realities, but Thackeray uses the ready-made social symbol very quietly. It is his great gift, here and elsewhere, to work through a plenitude of such unobtrusively significant action, and not only each detail of pedagogy, teaching and learning, but every single aspect of the scene, events and characters, in this first chapter, is morally expressive.

One key to the theme of art and nature is given in the first image, which contrasts the undignified with the dignified. It does so in a way which draws our attention to the narrow formality of the institution which Becky and Amelia are about to leave for the wide world. The fat horses and the fat coachman, the bandy-legged servant and the red nose of Miss Jemima Pinkerton represent the vivid, undignified informal world, while 'the great iron gate of Miss Pinkerton's academy for young ladies' represents dignity and enclosure. The contrast becomes plainer in the first piece of dialogue between Miss Pinkerton and her sister Miss Jemima, who are a contrasting pair in a novel largely organized on the principle of contrast and duality. The contrast emerges as one of style and sensibility, directing our attention to Miss Jemima's natural, informal, good-hearted, outer-directed attention and the formality and arrangement of Miss Pinkerton's artifice:

'It is Mrs Sedley's coach, sister,' said Miss Jemima. 'Sambo, the black servant, has just rung the bell; and the coachman has a new red waistcoat.'
'Have you completed all the necessary preparations incident

to Miss Sedley's departure, Miss Jemima?' asked Miss Pinkerton
herself. . . . (Chap. 1)

Miss Jemima speaks loosely, but has her eye on the colours
and particulars of the world outside. Her concreteness is indeed
characteristic of Thackeray's descriptions, and throughout the
novel his eye is fixed on the solidity and detail of persons,
clothing and objects; his presentation of Amelia and Becky, for
instance, is marked by this precision, of action and colour. Here,
the concreteness makes Miss Jemima interesting, while her sister
is less attractive in her dryness and abstraction of style. The
Johnsonian lady, Miss Pinkerton, speaks in the grand style; she
is presented appropriately by Thackeray in polysyllabic, allusive
and high-piled grandeur, as he sets the linguistic tone for the
ensuing dialogue: 'Miss Pinkerton herself, that majestic lady;
the Semiramis of Hammersmith, the friend of Dr Johnson, the
correspondent of Mrs Chapone herself.' His grand style acts as
a faint burlesque, not pushing its effects, but maintaining grandeur of vocabulary and syntax. The contrast between the sisters
becomes explicit when Miss Jemima uses the old word 'bowpot'
and is told to say 'bouquet' as more genteel, doing her best in
the compromise of 'booky', which is followed up by the big-
hearted but undignified simile, 'as big almost as a haystack'.
The sisters' styles draw attention to the formality and pedantry
of the one and the clumsy and casual artlessness of the other;
and throughout Thackeray works in circumlocutions, like
'autograph letter' or 'billet', and in typically Johnsonian figures
of sentiments and negation, parallelism and more periodic
elaboration,[1] all shown paradigmatically in this model letter:

---

[1] Comparison of Thackeray's portrait of Miss Pinkerton with the language
and sentiments of Samuel Johnson suggests that Thackeray had Johnson
close at hand. Amelia is 'not unworthy' of assuming social position; Johnson
describes Swift's advancement similarly: 'In the year following he wrote
A Project for the Advancement of Religion, addressed to Lady Berkeley, by
whose kindness it is not unlikely that he was advanced to benefices.' (*Life
of Swift*, para. 34)
    In the second sentence of Miss Pinkerton's letter, Thackeray parodies
the parallelisms and movement from general to particular of a typical
Johnsonian sentence: 'Milton would not have excelled in dramatick
writing; he knew human nature only in the gross, and had never studied
the shades of character, nor the combinations of concurring or the perplexity
of contending passions.' (*Life of Milton*, para. 268)

MADAM, – After her six years' residence at the Mall, I have the honour and happiness of presenting Miss Amelia Sedley to her parents, as a young lady not unworthy to occupy a fitting position in their polished and refined circle. Those virtues which characterise the young English gentlewoman, those accomplishments which become her birth and station, will not be found wanting in the amiable Miss Sedley, whose *industry* and *obedience* have endeared her to her instructors, and whose delightful sweetness of temper has charmed her *aged* and her *youthful* companions.

In music, in dancing, in orthography, in every variety of embroidery and needle-work, she will be found to have realised her friends' *fondest wishes*. In geography there is still much to be desired; and a careful and undeviating use of the backboard, for four hours daily during the next three years, is recommended as necessary to the acquirement of that dignified *deportment* and *carriage*, so requisite for every young lady of *fashion*. (Ibid.)

What is said is as important as how it is said, but style and value are related. Miss Pinkerton's careful and pedantic 'For whom is this, Miss Jemima?' is answered by the artless and warm-hearted 'For Becky Sharp: she's going too', which undermines the style and the very insistence of Miss Pinkerton's question. Thackeray works through dialogue and through the surrounding narration and description. The humanity of Miss Jemima's unpedantic, unpremeditated natural style matches her spontaneous show of sensibility: she trembles, blushes all over 'her withered face and neck', and her sensibility shows itself in her wasted imaginative identification with Becky, 'it's only two and ninepence and poor Becky will be miserable if she don't get one'. Miss Jemima, like Briggs later on, is much too simple-minded to criticize the grand and acquisitive cold-heartedness

---

And Miss Pinkerton's pedagogical advice to Amelia regarding '*deportment* and *carriage*' echoes Johnson's account of Swift's failure as a student very faithfully: 'It must disappoint every reader's expectation that, when at the usual time he claimed the Bachelorship of Arts, he was found by the examiners too conspicuously deficient for regular admission, and obtained his degree at last by special favour, a term used in that university to denote want of merit.

'Of this disgrace it may easily be supposed that he was much ashamed, and shame had its proper effect in producing reformation. He resolved from that time to study eight-hours a day, and continued his industry for seven years, with what improvement is sufficiently known.' (Ibid., paras 415-16)

around her, but her criticism is implicit in the language and feelings. Predatory Miss Pinkerton is coldly, self-interestedly and manipulatively in control, in giving, speaking, teaching and writing; Miss Jemima is vulgar, loving, giving, artlessly betrayed by feeling and undignified in action and speech, trotting off, ungrandly, 'exceedingly flurried and nervous'. Miss Pinkerton's condolence is a public event: ' . . . Once, when poor Miss Birch died of the scarlet fever, was Miss Pinkerton known to write personally to the parents of her pupils; and it was Jemima's opinion that if anything *could* console Mrs Birch for her daughter's loss, it would be that pious and eloquent composition in which Miss Pinkerton announced the event.'

From the beginning, therefore, Thackeray establishes a contrast between formal showing-off and lack of heart, loving generosity and lack of style. He also establishes, from the beginning, a sense of social hierarchy and power-structure, not unrelated to the style and capacity for feeling. Those who are at the top, in Vanity Fair, get there by art, not heart. The linguistic and moral contrast between the 'superior' and the 'inferior' sister is followed by the contrast between two other ladies in the hierarchy, Becky and Amelia: 'Miss Sedley's papa was a merchant in London, and a man of some wealth; whereas Miss Sharp was an articled pupil, for whom Miss Pinkerton had done, as she thought, quite enough, without conferring upon her at parting the high honour of the Dixonary.' The psychological pecking-order can override the social,[2] as Thackeray demonstrates in the little passage in which Becky makes her 'adieux' in fluent French, unintelligible to Miss Pinkerton, thus inflicting a stylistic victory, appropriately enough, over the Johnsonian mode. This victory is accompanied by a flouting gesture, as Becky refuses to accept one of Miss Pinkerton's fingers: 'In fact, it was a little battle between the young lady and the old one, and the latter was worsted.' One could describe the whole action of the novel in such military terms, and Thackeray uses them freely; he is well aware of ironic parallels between his story and history, and also of the 'unheroic' appropriation of military or heroic terms to everyday strife. In his novels, these skirmishes are fought with social weapons – with words, sentences, wit,

[2] For a fuller discussion of this kind of reversal, see Chap. 1.

foreign languages, gestures, rituals, refusal of ritual, clothes, presents. Thackeray does more than show Becky as victorious, her strength of personality, intelligence, and learning prevailing over her low place in the social order. He creates a contrast between failure and success in artifice and ritual. Miss Pinkerton makes her ridiculous, elaborate gesture, 'she waved one hand, both by way of adieu, and to give Miss Sharp an opportunity of shaking one of the fingers of the hand which was left out for that purpose', and Becky nonchalantly rejects it. Becky's very last gesture, however, is not an act of social aggression against the style of the Hammersmith Semiramis, but a rejection of poor loving styleless Jemima. The throwing of the dictionary is of course a marvellous rejection of style – Johnson, the institution, order, dignity and pretence – but it is not a simple revolutionary gesture which we can applaud. As so often, Becky is on the wrong side, attacking the Establishment only because she is jealous of its advantages. Our sympathies are carefully withdrawn from her as she throws back what is not only a symbol of 'corrupt' style, but a loving present. Miss Jemima's very last speech and action are typically artless, broken and stammered, and her last generous, if silly, act, is accompanied by the words, 'God bless you!' Becky, like Scrooge, rejects a blessing. The rejection marks her entry into the great world.

Thackeray's last sentences emphasize the contrast between the world of school and the great world, as the gates close; he says, formally, 'and so, farewell to Chiswick Mall'. The brilliant close-up of this first scene has established style and theme, the style and theme of nature and art.

There are certain characters in this chapter I have not mentioned, and they too are involved in style and theme. They are the author and his readers, real and imaginary. Before the curtain rises, in 'Before the Curtain', Thackeray has presented himself as the Manager of the Performance; he has begun to develop the histrionic significance, as well as the vanity and commerce of Vanity Fair; he has admitted that he is in it for money, and is not without charlatanry: amongst the crowd he singles out 'quacks (*other* quacks, plague take them!)'.[3] The

---

[3] In the frontispiece, not only is 'the moralist who is holding forth on the cover' wearing a fool's cap, but so is every member of his audience, even including a mother and her baby.

author is, from the beginning, involved in the business of art and acting.[4] As we know, Thackeray originally intended to call the novel 'A Novel without a Hero' and to develop the theme of unheroic drama, rather than that of Vanity Fair. Although there are divergent emphases, the two themes very plainly overlap, and in Thackeray's claim to the unheroic, he uses the convention of the self-conscious artist to make a certain claim for realism. A certain claim : implicit in his insistence that this is art, that these are puppets, that this is illusion and performance, that it is a book, written for money by an author, and read by various readers, is the claim that it is closer to life and nature than some forms of art. The self-conscious claim to realism is made in the description of Amelia's undignified, unheroinelike beauty and sensibility. Another complex claim for heart as against art, it ends with a disarming address to a Reader, Jones, whose taste is 'for the great and heroic in life and novels' and who will underline the author's 'foolish, twaddling, etc.', and add *'quite true'*. But Jones is critically presented as a worldling, reading at his club, and 'rather flushed with his joint of mutton and half-pint of wine', and it seems likely that Thackeray uses him in order to further the claim for simple, unworldly heroines and passions. He does as much as he can to claim that his novel, though a work of art, has a heart, and not simply by making jokes about the wrong kind of heartless, art-seeking (but wine-flushed) reader like Jones, but by deliberately drawing attention to his own sentimentality. Amelia has a heart, cries over silly novels, and dead pets, and attracts heart : in yet another qualification of the pecking-order, even Semiramis gives orders that Amelia should be treated gently, and when Amelia goes she is surrounded by loving, giving, weeping friends. Indeed, Becky is not entirely the victim of the class hierarchy, since Amelia's friends are seen to love her for herself ('kindly, smiling, tender, gentle, generous heart') and perhaps even Miss Pinkerton is not sensitive to her wholly because of her father's income. Though Becky is made to claim, in Chapter 2, 'In Which Miss Sharp and Miss Sedley Prepare to Open the Campaign', that

---

[4] 'Before the Curtain' was written by Thackeray after he wrote the novel, for its publication in book form. It appeared in the last number of the serial publication. For more on this subject and the precedents for the dramatic analogy, see Joan Stevens, 'A Note on Thackeray's Manager of the Performance', *NCF*, 22 (March 1968), 391-7.

Amelia was her only friend, we shall, in retrospect, blame that on Becky's heartlessness rather than on the social hierarchy of the school. Jones's rejection of Amelia is made to be a rejection of sentimentality, and Thackeray lays claim to the sentimental as an index of sensibility: she cries over dead pets, lost friends, and even silly novels. Thackeray makes it awkward for us by linking the three so that we cannot be as selective in our emotional snobbishness as we should like.

Amelia is, as a character and a woman, deliberately senti-mental: that is, she is meant to be the sentimental heroine of an unsentimental novel, illustrating the complexity of the heart's excesses. We shall begin by loving her and feeling with her, in her friendship, love, grief, maternal affection, but we shall eventually learn the limitations of sensibility uncontrolled by reason: she will worship her unworthy husband, alive and dead, spoil her son, and make sentimental demands on Dobbin, her patient lover. The very first chapter prepares us for this aspect of Thackeray's criticism, his refusal to accept unqualified sen-sibility as a moral norm. Heart like this can be linked with silliness and excess: it is all very well to cry for dead birds but not for silly novels. But the qualification of heart is less con-spicuous, at first, than the qualification of art. Only in the misplaced loving gift of Miss Jemima, the rejected dictionary, do we see our first clear instance of sentimentality; it is punished rudely by its exact opposite, hard-heartedness, which also earns its first clear criticism when, biting the hand that feeds, it throws back the dictionary at the silly affectionate old woman. The reader is involved even with her rejection, because Thackeray tells us, drily, that she is not going to appear again :

. . . Miss Jemima had already whimpered several times at the idea of Amelia's departure; and, but for fear of her sister, would have gone off in downright hysterics, like the heiress (who paid double) of St Kitt's. Such luxury of grief, however, is only allowed to parlour-boarders. Honest Jemima had all the bills, and the washing, and the mending, and the puddings, and the plate and crockery, and the servants to superintend. But why speak about her? It is probable that we shall not hear of her again from this moment to the end of time, and that when the great filigree iron gates are once closed on her, she and her awful sister will never issue therefrom into this little world of history. (Ibid.)

What does this rather odd passage mean? That there are heroines even less heroic than Amelia, who is, once this passage has urged us to reflect, more of a heroine than Miss Jemima? Thackeray seems to mean what he says in the sentence 'Such luxury of grief, however, is only allowed to parlour-boarders'. In a novel which is about the luxury of grief, Thackeray reminds us, in the dismissal of Jemima, of the circumstances that permit grief, in and out of novels. He also claims for his novel a high degree of realism; though it is interesting to distinguish his claim from George Eliot's in the totally tolerant *Adam Bede*, where Lizbeth Bede *is* permitted her 'luxury of grief'. At the same time, he draws our attention to the social interest of his emotional theme: if people like Amelia dwell on grief, devote themselves to worship of dead husband and living son, it is as a luxury. Thus he makes another qualification of heart: sensitivity, as well as art, depends on position and possessions. Thackeray's initial creation of category is uncomfortably blurred. On the one hand we have Miss Pinkerton, the Johnsonian style, the great filigree iron gates, Jones, with his contempt for sentiment, and Becky, able to put down the grand style with fluent French. On the other hand, Amelia, all tolerant and sentimental readers, and Jemima, loving, giving, artless. Between the two worlds, the rejection of the dictionary; yet, beside it, Jemima's blessing and the two-edged admission that Jemima is not promising material for Thackeray's novel.

The realistic effects of the self-conscious reference should be stressed here. Thackeray insists on the illusion, the art, the performance, the drama, the novel, but in such a way – dismissing a character who is not qualified to be a character – that brings the novel very close indeed to life. There are some unpromising materials, he says, that will not come in; and the very mention reminds us of the novelist's selection from life, in a way that is moving and evaluative. At the extreme of art is Thackeray himself; at the extreme of heart is Jemima, who will be left out. The reader is made wary, and perhaps, as Thackeray wished, uncomfortable. If he is attentive, he will not reject Jones, Amelia, Miss Pinkerton or Johnson's dictionary too precipitately.

This first formal and framing scene in Chapter 1 of *Vanity Fair* makes plain the heroines' initiation into the great world, and the reader's initiation into the world of the novel. In Chapter 8, Thackeray draws our attention, first by direct dramatic presentation, then by complex authorial commentary, to certain crucial differences between Becky's art and his own. In the chapters that bridge the initiation and the very explicit analysis, we have seen Becky beginning her career as an artist in life. She does, in fact, possess some positive artistic talents, chiefly displayed in her entertaining and persuasive performances of miming and singing. In Chapter 8, Thackeray adds a new artistic achievement, epistolary and literary. Becky's letter to Amelia probably takes a glance at epistolary fiction in its feminine effusiveness and self-pity, and its very lack of resemblance to the situations of Pamela and Clarissa. But the chief purpose, as I see it, is to bridge Becky's artistic forte, which is dramatic, and Thackeray's, which is literary.

Becky is given the whole narrative burden, for the space of her letter, of introducing the reader to a new place and several new characters. She is a quite convenient surrogate for Thackeray, being, like him, sharply attentive, witty and satirical, but she is of course not simply a surrogate, and her letter also shows the Becky Sharp traits of false sensibility and predatoriness. Her letters are usually written to get something, directly or indirectly, and this letter is clearly designed to keep a tenuous hook on the Sedleys – 'Is your poor brother recovered of his rack-punch?' – and even Amelia, who may be good for another India muslin or pink silk in the future. But the cast-off dresses are still fresh (see Chapter 11 for the hint about their replacements) and Thackeray is free to develop Becky's literary gifts.

Throughout the novel, her letters are important in the furthering of the action and the development of her character. There is the unsuccessful letter dictated to Rawdon and addressed to Miss Crawley, which does not take in the old lady for a minute, since Becky has thought of using short sentences but not of mis-spelling. Moreover, the letter is fatally amusing, and Miss Crawley detects Becky's fundamental style, as well as appreciating it and asking for more. There is the more crucial letter written to Rawdon in the sponging-house, designed to put him off affectionately and humorously, but unable to hide her exhibitionism and self-interest. Its crude ingratiation does not

take in Rawdon, who also detects her fundamental style, failing
to be amused by Becky's jokes, and disliking them for the first
time. But the first letter, in Chapter 8, is a more disengaged
venture. It introduces the reader to King's Crawley and to some
new and important characters. It is a superb stroke of art,
totally and variously eloquent. The very title of the chapter,
'Private and Confidential', is expressive of the epistolary gossip
of bosom-friends and its frank-mark, 'Free.-Pitt Crawley', is
informative and ironic – who pays and for what, or who does
not pay, is always of interest in Thackeray.

> My Dearest, Sweetest Amelia,
>   With what mingled joy and sorrow do I take up the pen to
> write to my dearest friend! Oh, what a change between to-day
> and yesterday! *Now* I am friendless and alone; yesterday I was
> at home, in the sweet company of a sister, whom I shall ever,
> *ever* cherish!
>   I will not tell you in what tears and sadness I passed the fatal
> night in which I separated from you. *You* went on Tuesday to
> joy and happiness, with your mother and *your devoted young
> soldier* by your side; and I thought of you all night, dancing at
> Perkins's, the prettiest, I am sure, of all the young ladies at the
> Ball. I was brought by the groom in the old carriage to Sir Pitt
> Crawley's town house, where, after John the groom had behaved
> most rudely and insolently to me (alas! 'twas safe to insult
> poverty and misfortune!), I was given over to Sir P's care, and
> made to pass the night in an old gloomy bed, and by the side
> of a horrid gloomy old charwoman, who keeps the house. I did
> not sleep one single wink the whole night.
>   Sir Pitt is not what we silly girls, when we used to read Cecilia
> at Chiswick, imagined a baronet must have been. Anything,
> indeed, less like Lord Orville cannot be imagined. Fancy an old,
> stumpy, short, vulgar, and very dirty man, in old clothes and
> shabby old gaiters, who smokes a horrid pipe, and cooks his own
> horrid supper in a saucepan. He speaks with a country accent,
> and swore a great deal at the old charwoman, at the hackney
> coachman who drove us to the inn where the coach went from,
> and on which I made the journey *outside for the greater part
> of the way.* . . .
>   'There's an avenue,' said Sir Pitt, 'a mile long. There's six
> thousand pound of timber in them there trees. Do you call that
> nothing?' He pronounced avenue – *eveneu*, and nothing –
> *nothink*, so droll. . . .

Here, my dear, I was interrupted last night by a dreadful thumping at my door; and who do you think it was? Sir Pitt Crawley in his night-cap and dressing gown, such a figure! As I shrank away from such a visitor, he came forward and seized my candle; 'no candles after eleven o'clock, Miss Becky,' said he. 'Go to bed in the dark, you pretty little hussey (that is what he called me), and unless you wish me to come for the candle every night, mind and be in bed at eleven.' And with this, he and Mr Horrocks the butler went off laughing. You may be sure I shall not encourage any more of their visits. They let loose two immense blood-hounds at night, which all last night were yelling and howling at the moon. . . .

Half an hour after our arrival, the great dinner-bell was rung, and I came down with my two pupils (they are very thin and insignificant little chits of ten and eight years old). I came down in your *dear* muslin gown (about which that odious Mrs Pinner was so rude, because you gave it me); for I am to be treated as one of the family, except on company days, when the young ladies and I are to dine up-stairs.

Well, the great dinner-bell rang, and we all assembled in the little drawing-room where my Lady Crawley sits. She is the second Lady Crawley, and mother of the young ladies. She was an ironmonger's daughter, and her marriage was thought a great match. She looks as if she had been handsome once, and her eyes are always weeping for the loss of her beauty. She is pale and meagre, and high-shouldered; and has not a word to say for herself, evidently. Her step-son, Mr Crawley, was likewise in the room. He was in full dress, as pompous as an undertaker. He is pale, thin, ugly, silent; he has thin legs, no chest, hay-coloured whiskers, and straw-coloured hair. He is the very picture of his sainted mother over the mantel-piece – Griselda of the noble house of Binkie. . . .

Lady Crawley is always knitting the worsted. Sir Pitt is always tipsy, every night; and, I believe, sits with Horrocks, the butler. Mr Crawley always reads sermons in the evening; and in the morning is locked up in his study, or else rides to Mudbury, on county business, or to Squashmore, where he preaches, on Wednesdays and Fridays, to the tenants there.

A hundred thousand grateful loves to your dear papa and mamma! Is your poor brother recovered of his rack-punch? Oh, dear! Oh, dear! How men should beware of wicked punch!

Ever and ever thine own,
REBECCA

The first thing we notice is the conventional satire on female sensibility. The strongest impression is that of exaggeration and falsity: 'My Dearest, Sweetest Amelia'; or 'With what mingled joy and sorrow do I take up the pen to write to my dearest friend! . . . Now I am friendless and alone. . . .' But these initial emotions of indulgence, envy and self-pity soon give way to the sheer verve of narrative and presentation of character. Thackeray does something simple but clever with Becky's narration; he allows it to overlap slightly with his own narrative in Chapter 10, so that we see a slight discrepancy between what has happened and what Becky presents as happening. Nothing very marked; just a little evidence that Becky is a liar: the detail that she has not slept a wink (when the author has said that she does) and the omission of her attempt to pump the old charwoman with whom she shares a bed. She presents herself as the heroine of a Gothic novel[5] rather than a resilient, unfastidious and predatory opportunist. But what is most striking is the wit and humour of Becky's narrative, achieved at the expense of the characters in her story. The girls are 'very thin and insignificant little chits of ten and eight years old'. Lady Crawley 'looks as if she had been handsome once, and her eyes are always weeping for the loss of her beauty'. Pitt Crawley is 'pompous as an undertaker . . . pale, thin, ugly, silent; he has thin legs, no chest, hay-coloured whiskers, and straw-coloured hair'. Sir Pitt is exposed by his 'dumpy little legs' and rustic accent. The butler is laughed at for his ludicrous French pronunciation (Becky's pride in her French is one of her humourless weaknesses), and Miss Horrocks, descibed as 'very much overdressed', flings Becky a look of scorn as 'she plumped down on her knees'.

Such strokes of wit and ridicule may be enjoyed for their own sake, and our critical spirit may be held in check until Thackeray himself stands back to analyse the letter. The contrast between the maidenly gush and the hard-hitting satire is probably clear, but we do not feel strongly critical until Thackeray drily observes that we should.[6] For although he has been using Becky

[5] It is like a burlesque of Richardson in parts, of Mrs Radcliffe in others.
[6] See Edgar F. Harden, 'The Discipline and Significance of Form in *Vanity Fair*', *PMLA*, 82 (December 1967), 530-42. Harden shows that *Vanity Fair* has a thoroughgoing pattern that specifically pairs and groups successive instalments.

as a narrator, the narration is itself material for satire. It is satire proffered for the reader's enjoyment, then analysed by the satirist.

Everything considered, I think it is quite as well for our dear Amelia Sedley, in Russell Square, that Miss Sharp and she are parted. Rebecca is a droll funny creature, to be sure; and those descriptions of the poor lady weeping for the loss of her beauty, and the gentleman 'with hay-coloured whiskers and straw-coloured hair', are very smart, doubtless, and show a great knowledge of the world. That she might, when on her knees, have been thinking of something better than Miss Horrocks's ribbons, has possibly struck both of us. But my kind reader will please to remember, that this history has 'Vanity Fair' for a title, and that Vanity Fair is a very vain, wicked, foolish place, full of all sorts of humbugs and falsenesses and pretensions. And while the moralist, who is holding forth on the cover (an accurate portrait of your humble servant), professes to wear neither gown nor bands, but only the very same long-eared livery in which his congregation is arrayed : yet, look you, one is bound to speak the truth as far as one knows it, whether one mounts a cap and bells or a shovel-hat; and a deal of disagreeable matter must come out in the course of such an undertaking. (Chap. 8)

This first ironic combination of criticism and defence is Thackeray at his most subtle and disconcerting : we cannot know what he is saying in this first paragraph which neatly balances indictment with justification, and relates Becky to her author. But what does he mean by speaking the truth? Does he refer to his own exposure of Becky? Or does he also include her exposure of the vanity and foolishness of Lady Crawley, Pitt and Miss Horrocks, who are all easily and accurately describable as vain and foolish, 'full of all sorts of humbugs and falsenesses and pretensions'.

Another contrast and symmetrical figure follow : the story of a preacher – a Neapolitan story-teller – who worked himself up into such a 'rage and passion' against 'some of the villains whose wicked deeds he was describing and inventing that the audience could not resist it'. The result of the story-teller's fervour was a good profit : 'the hat went round, and the bajocchi tumbled into it, in the midst of a perfect storm of sympathy'. This anecdote is balanced against that of the Parisian actors who refuse to play villains and prefer to play virtuous characters for a lower payment.[7] He observes : 'I set these two stories one against the other, so that you may see that it is not from mere mercenary motives that the present performer is desirous to show up and trounce his villains; but because he has a sincere hatred of them, which he cannot keep down, and which must find a vent in suitable abuse and bad language.' Not a simple antithesis, it needs careful analysis before we finally conclude that Thackeray is admitting his own lack of pure motivation. After all, he is a performer who gains from the performance, an author earning his living with this serial (later a book) which is paid for by the reader. Thackeray is distinguishing between his satiric stance and Becky's; he is telling us clearly that though a critic, she is subjected to the author's criticism as 'one who has no reverence except for prosperity, and no eye for anything beyond success. Such people there are living and flourishing in the world – Faithless, Hopeless, Charityless; let us have at them, dear friends, with might and main'.

This disclosure criticizes and clarifies Becky's wit and ridicule. While admitting that Thackeray writes for gain, it claims that his satiric mode derives from Faith, Hope and Charity. It invokes lofty and noble moral purpose : he is mercenary but not 'merely' mercenary. If we then look at Thackeray's irony, scorn, wit and ridicule, we see that his satire is not cynical; rather it derives from Hope and Faith in the possibilities of human nature, and has Charity. Thackeray is a master of timing and placing, and follows this criticism of Becky's immoral and eclectic satire and wit by a conspicuously charitable and serious satiric piece in the next chapter. Another instance of symmetry and juxtaposition, it is also an instance of Thackeray's explicitness and clarity. Uncomfortable though he may be as a satirist constantly involving the reader in the satire, he takes no chances with misunderstanding. He is writing a novel about the corruption of nature, and this corruption shows itself here, in Becky, performance, wit and satire. However, as an artist sharing the actions of performance, wit and satire, he is constrained to distinguish between right and wrong wit, right and wrong satire. The distinctions

[7] Thackeray was very impressed by this evidence of moral action in the theatre and wrote about it first in more detail in *The Paris Sketch-Book*.

involve an art which has a heart – Hope, Faith, Charity – and an art which is heartless, 'no reverence for anything except for prosperity'. At the same time, he is aware and forced to admit that he is involved in profiting too. The character and the author are fully compared and contrasted. This is extremely rare in English fiction, apart from the earlier and influential case of Fielding who presented, in *Tom Jones*, antithetical images of his own desire for lofty Fame and worldly prosperity – what

Thackeray, memorably recalling Fielding's invocation of roast beef, calls 'a little of the Sunday side'.

Chapter 8, then, exposes Becky as a heartless artist practising Thackeray's arts, and implies that Thackeray is more honourable than Becky. Chapter 9 follows with a demonstration, taking a revised look at those characters analysed so heartlessly and artfully by Becky. Sir Pitt, Lady Crawley and Mr Pitt Crawley are all presented afresh, with wit and satire, and with sympathy and charity. Sir Pitt, for whom admittedly little can be said, is shown as first marrying 'under the auspices of his parents', then marrying to please himself. There is feeling in 'He had his pretty Rose, and what more need a man require than to please himself?' What follows is inside information, not mere brilliant superficial wit, and it is much more devastating than Becky's exposure:

c

'So he used to get drunk every night : to beat his pretty Rose sometimes : to leave her in Hampshire when he went to London for the parliamentary session, without a single friend in the whole world.' An extremely charitable account of pretty Rose herself follows, together with a glance at her limitations and losses : ' . . . she had no sort of character, nor talents, nor opinions, nor occupations, nor amusements, nor that vigour of soul and ferocity of temper which often falls to the lot of entirely foolish women. . . . O Vanity Fair – Vanity Fair ! This might have been, but for you, a cheery lass : – Peter Butt and Rose, a happy man and wife'.

There is a dignified and sympathetic account of Pitt, his respect for his mother-in-law, his kindness, and then – just in case we were beginning to identify Thackeray's manner of satiric analysis with charity and imagination – a devastating account of his mediocrity, industry and lack of self-knowledge. Thackeray's own wit is disarmingly produced when least expected, as we nod over his ability to see the humanity of these characters with heart and generosity; it is harder than anything achieved by Becky's rather visual ridicule : '. . . yet he failed somehow, in spite of a mediocrity which ought to have insured any man a success. He did not even get the prize poem, which all his friends said he was sure of'. Thackeray is very deliberate in his revision of Becky's satire, even to the extent of commenting when he agrees with her : 'Miss Sharp's accounts of his employment at Queen's Crawley were not caricatures. He subjected the servants there to the devotional exercises before mentioned, in which (and so much the better) he brought his father to join.' The parentheses of course mark, once more, the comment Becky would not be capable of making.

Thackeray's expansion and revision has one last effect. He has a capacity for moral and social diagnosis and generalization which Becky, at least at this stage in her education, utterly lacks. She sees, at school and out of it, how she is at an unfair disadvantage because of her birth and poverty; but later, when she makes the celebrated suggestion that she could be a good woman on five thousand a year, she does not see into the heartlessness of Vanity Fair, having insufficient heart and vision for the enterprise. Her social criticism, even when generalized, is shallow. Thackeray, having like Becky observed Sir Pitt's drunkenness

and illiteracy, though more seriously and less amusedly, also sees
the criticism of society involved in marking the defects of this
dignitary. Becky finds Sir Pitt funny; 'Anything, indeed, less like
Lord Orville cannot be imagined,' she comments, in her literary
and hypocritically fastidious way. Thackeray replaces this with
a moral fervour :

> Vanity Fair – Vanity Fair! Here was a man, who could not
> spell, and did not care to read – who had the habits and the
> cunning of a boor : whose aim in life was pettifogging : who
> never had a taste, or emotion, or enjoyment, but what was sordid
> and foul; and yet he had rank, and honours, and power,
> somehow : and was a dignitary of the land, and a pillar of the
> state. He was high sheriff, and rode in a golden coach. Great
> ministers and statesmen courted him; and in Vanity Fair he had
> a higher place than the most brilliant genius or spotless virtue.
> (Chap. 9)

At one stroke, Thackeray candidly admits his own involve-
ment; he makes explicit and dramatic the seriousness, profundity
and passion of his satire. Avoiding a simple division of intellect
or feeling into art and nature, he creates an art which is as close
to nature, and as inclusive and serious, as possible. He also
suggests, craftily and dramatically, that social criticism is his
aim.

CHAPTER THREE

Performance for Profit

And moreover, at this Fair there is at all times
to be seen Jugglings, cheats, games, plays, fools,
apes, knaves, and rogues, and that of all sorts.
The Pilgrim's Progress

Ye nymphs of rosy lips and radiant eyes,
Whom Pleasure keeps too busy to be wise,
Whom Joys with soft varieties invite,
By day the frolick, and the dance by night,
Who frown with vanity, who smile with art,
And ask the latest fashion of the heart.
Samuel Johnson, 'The Vanity of Human Wishes'

Thackeray suggests in a letter that he could be a good man on
ten thousand a year: and he could certainly have adapted
Flaubert and said, 'Becky Sharp, c'est moi'. This identification
is an incomplete one, of course. Becky, like Pendennis or Blanche
or Clive or the Bachelor in *Lovel the Widower*, is only a fragmentary and provisional selection from Thackeray's personal
experience. But there are certain characters with whom he seems
closely identified, though in a way which holds none of the
obvious emotional gratifications of realism or fantasy. With
characters like Becky, Blanche and Pen in certain modes and
moods, and even with the Fotheringay, he is identified in an
unusually professional way with their performance. An essential
part of this identification involves the recognition that performance is profitable. Bingley, 'great in the character of the Stranger',
determined to 'fascinate' Pendennis and Foker 'for he knew they
had paid their money'. Pen begins his career in journalism by
writing verses to illustrate a picture of the Church Porch, which
has to be printed and poetically illustrated because 'the governor

68

gave sixty pounds' for the plate. Pendennis, as the fictitious author of *The Adventures of Philip*, is 'lost in a respectful astonishment' as he reflects that each word brings in the money :

> With the words 'Ah, how wonderful' to the words 'per line', 1 can buy a loaf, a piece of butter, a jug of milk, a modicum of tea, – actually enough to make breakfast for the family; and the servants of the house; and the charwoman, *their* servant, can shake up the tea-leaves with a fresh supply of water, sop the crusts, and get a meal, *tant bien que mal*. Wife, children, guests, servants, charwoman, we are all actually making a meal of Philip Firmin's bones as it were. (Chap. 16)

Gordon Ray quotes a contemporary reviewer's verdict, 'surely this is the strangest way in the world to interest or amuse people', but it is certainly a way very typical of Thackeray, and central to his moral satire. He enjoys plays with layers of fiction and illusion, every bit as much as Sterne or Beckett, and like theirs, his is a serious play. From the beginning to the end of his career he is concerned to blur the distinction between satirist and subject, acutely aware of the superior stance which is structurally conferred on the author, and anxious to disclaim it. His anxiety is quite plain, I believe, once we recognize his interest in performance and profit. In *Vanity Fair*, *Pendennis* and *Philip* he is concerned with money and the lack of it, with extremes of wealth and poverty, and with the corruptions of human love and creativity by need and greed. He knows that need and greed shade into each other, and defines them, and the shady area where they meet, in detailed terms of prices and market values, pounds, shillings and pence. We know how much the Sedleys paid for style, how much Foker paid for his dreary dinner at Richmond, how much Pen got for those verses which he wrote when he was down to his last five-pound note. The details of prices are characteristic of Thackeray's social concreteness and very important in his definitions of professionalism and prostitution. We also know about the high price Becky got from Lord Steyne, though we are less certain about what he bought. Beside acknowledging that art brought in money, and often took direction from need, Thackeray wanted to describe the acquisitive society in considerable detail. He intended to reveal the actual corruptions of performance.

As so often with Thackeray, we have to make careful qualifications. Although he was criticized for his criticisms of Grub
Street, he was too long a journalist and too perceptive and
tolerant a human being to be an intellectual snob. Geoffrey
Tillotson quotes approvingly that moving passage in *Pendennis*
where the author says that the Kotzebue play is trash, but that
trash can have a heart :

> Nobody ever talked so. If we meet idiots in life, as will happen,
> it is a great mercy that they do not use such absurdly fine words.
> The Stranger's talk is sham, like the book he reads, and the
> hair he wears, and the bank he sits on, and the diamond ring
> he makes play with – but, in the midst of the balderdash, there
> runs that reality of love, children, and forgiveness of wrong,
> which will be listened to wherever it is preached, and sets all the
> world sympathising. (Chap. 4)

Or, to adapt Noël Coward, 'Strange how potent cheap drama is'.
Thackeray knows that the difference between Nature and Art
is not easy to establish, since both good and bad Art may possess
Nature. He had critical standards in literary judgment, and
rejected Micawber, for instance, as typical of Dickens's lack of
realism, but it seems important to recognize that his tolerance
extended to 'balderdash' and to see why. Such tolerance suggests
that he had some sympathy for Amelia's tears over silly novels,
and rather less for the more sophisticated tastes of Jones.

My immediate concern is not so much with Thackeray's
literary taste and judgment as with his interest in art. While
accepting that art is a business, and does involve traffic and trade,
he rejects the corrupt art which is purely heartless, simply
exhibitionist, and exists solely to make money. Let me briefly
recall Thackeray's personal experience, early expectations, his
extravagance as a young man, the loss of his fortune,[1] and his
gradual assumption of the profession of journalist and novelist.
He describes himself in a letter as 'a penny-a-liner and a diner'
and as we move through his intensely practical, busy and good-
tempered account of making a way in early-Victorian Grub
Street, we are divided between marvelling at his social energy
and at his hard work. He was much slower at writing profitably

[1] *Life*, Vol. 1, pp. 162-3.

than Dickens, and we find for many years a constant counting up of pounds and pence, especially in his correspondence with his mother, Mrs Carmichael Smith. There are hundreds of letters that show his awareness of having to provide for his children as well as for himself. He discusses, for instance, the need to keep a manservant, a maid and a cook, when the Carlyles manage with only one maid, but argues that he requires the man to run errands, and the cook and maid (not to mention a series of un-Jane Eyre-like governesses) for Anny and Minny, his daughters. His savouring of prosperity, when it came, shows the thoughtfulness and appreciation of a man who has had to count his pence. His long-standing resentment of the meanness of Mrs Shawe, his mother-in-law, exposed and punished in several devastating portraits, but most circumstantially in *Philip*, his rueful analysis of extravagance, his interest in frugality, and his constant awareness of prices, costs and values, reflect his professional struggle to earn.

It had to be performance for profit. His performance was usually not dramatic, but involved impersonation, in essays, stories and verse, generally comic and satiric. If Thackeray was very conscious of the financial pressures, he was also conscious of the social and personal ones. When Bulwer Lytton and Lever protested at being guyed in *Novels by Eminent Hands*, Thackeray was fully aware that he was criticizing fellow-writers, as he felt he had every right to do, and for money.[2] His correspondence reveals his considerable scrupulousness: far from being the heartless satirist or charlatan he was sometimes accused of being – one thinks of the celebrated jibe by Forster that he was 'false as hell' – he emerges as a professional writer extremely conscious that every lampoon, burlesque or review was strictly limited in disinterestedness. He might claim a moral and intellectual detachment for his criticism, but the plain fact he faced at every turn was that it was lucrative.

Because of need and conscientious reflection, he came to insist that he was in the Fair too, that he was mercenary, like Becky, though not 'merely' so. The insistence is made in a literary way in *Vanity Fair*, where the author-character, though like the Thackeray of the letters, is fragmentary, flexible, provisional; possessed of children in one place, and childless in

[2] *Letters*, Vol. II, p. 270.

another; with a named aunt and wife here, anonymous relatives there; with a striking ability, on the same page, to fool around – 'there are some terrific chapters coming' – and to adopt the grave accents of the sermon or polemic. It is an eclectic figure, itself a virtuoso performance, shifting roles with the mercurial adaptability of an Elizabethan character-actor, or a character designed for virtuoso performer, Face, Brainworm or Edgar. The adaptability and shape-changing is also traditionally expected of the mountebank or quack at the fair.

No one can fail to notice this shape-changing in the author-character. However, in both his virtuosity and in its profitability his close resemblance to Becky should be recognized. Thackeray's range is like Bunyan's, and includes all manner of performance and performers, 'jugglings, cheats, games, plays, fools, apes, knaves, and rogues, and that of all sorts'. *Vanity Fair* is, of course, the novel most concerned with performance for profit. Its first performer is the Thackeray-jester-preacher on the barrel, in the frontispiece, who advertises four main topics – performance, entertainment, preaching and profit, and also probably reaches back figuratively to Swift's *Tale of a Tub*, itself a masterpiece of self-conscious art, pastiche and ironic imperson-ation, though at a great remove from Thackeray's self-involved satire. Swift's Grub Street author telling a tale of a tub is not Swift and is condemned by Swift; Thackeray's author-character bears a very strong resemblance to Thackeray the man, and – more important – is a fictitious character respected, unlike Swift's author, for candour and self-criticism. After the preacher-jester appears the Manager of the Performance, artist, merchant and self-confessed quack, though with a heart. Next comes the first chapter of the novel, and the first stage, Miss Pinkerton's Academy, and its first performers, strictly amateur. Miss Pinker-ton is a performer, and performs for gain. Miss Pinkerton's Johnsonian testimonial is accompanied by a bill for ninety-three pounds, four shillings. But Miss Pinkerton is upstaged by Becky, even though Becky is as yet only an apprentice. In Chapter 2 Thackeray uses two phrases about her which are worth dwelling on. The first is not striking in itself : 'began to act for herself'. Here the literal sense of acting is revived by its context, and the implicit comparison with the first stages in her childish mimicry when, with 'the dismal precocity of poverty', she talked and turned away duns, and coaxed and wheedled tradesmen. Thackeray presents her as gifted, in wit and mimicry, and turning her gifts into a necessary trade. He also shows her encouraged and contaminated by her father's 'wild companions', performing the part of 'the ingénue' at Miss Pinkerton's, in order to get in, and putting on a different kind of act in burlesque and caricature at home. Thackeray deliberately seems to blur the distinction between performance as profession and as a way of life, and within that 'way of life' he shows us the performance as persuasive, self-advertising, deceptive and – a fine touch – socially contemptuous and subversive. At the Academy, Becky is also driven to act by loneliness and boredom, especially among women, then by envy, and last by a careful project of ambition : 'She determined at any rate to get free from the prison in which she found herself, and now began to act for herself and for the first time to make connected plans for the future.' As consciously as Stendhal's Julien Sorel, she educates herself for a social role, and is indeed one of the few characters[3] in the English Victorian novel who resemble the characters of Stendhal or Dostoevsky, in embarking deliberately and professionally on a role, in order to live profitably and interestingly in a society which she has analysed and understood. She equips herself, then blackmails Miss Pinkerton into finding her 'a good place as a governess in a nobleman's family'.

The first scene of her performance is in Amelia's house, and Thackeray stresses two things : her inexperience, as when she surprises Amelia by saying, unnecessarily, that she dotes on little children (a good psychological stroke on Thackeray's part, though he makes the liar go too far in lying), and her acquisitiveness, as she envies Amelia's things – 'her books, and her piano, and her dresses, and all her necklaces, brooches, laces and gimcracks'. In this novel, objects are dwelt on, as envied, used, acquired, bought, presented, and the result is to emphasize through them the conspicuous and histrionic consumption, and also their dramatic use. The bouquet and the dictionary, the dress and the white cornelian necklace, are very important properties in Becky's act.

Mostly Thackeray emphasizes the act itself : through the actual description of scenes of performance, such as the song,

---

[3] Others are Dickens's Uriah Heep and Gissing's Godwin Peake in *Born in Exile*.

'Ah, bleak and barren was the moor,' which is Thackeray's satiric version of the hymn about the poor orphan sung by Bessie in *Jane Eyre*, and by other songs and performances; by wit; by costume and property; and by a cumulative behaviouristic description which, contrasting very strongly with the inner action and feeling in other characters like Amelia or Dobbin, may act for a while, poker-faced and unobtrusively, but it strikes the attention sooner or later. By behaviouristic description, I mean the account of her controlled behaviour, confined to words, tones, gestures, and at times, as with a good actress, extending to laughter and even tears. Here are some examples from Chapter 4:

> 'I shan't have time to do it here,' said Rebecca. 'I'll do it when – when I'm gone.'

> 'For any one who wants a purse,' replied Miss Rebecca, looking at him in the most gentle winning way.

> [Miss Sharp's] 'deep-toned voice faltered'.

> 'Oh heavenly, heavenly flowers!' exclaimed Miss Sharp, and smelt them delicately, and held them to her bosom, and cast up her eyes to the ceiling in an ecstasy of admiration. Perhaps she just looked first into the bouquet, to see whether there was a *billet-doux* hidden among the flowers; but there was no letter.

Thackeray shows Becky arranging her language, tone, and behaviour, often simply doing things in appropriate emotional fashion, like entertaining her friends, or playing up to Jos in eating pineapple and chillies, or in talking about fascinating India, or in arranging her clothing and appearance to bring out her pathos and virginal lack of protection. 'Down stairs, then, they went, Joseph very red and blushing, Rebecca very modest, and holding her green eyes downwards. She was dressed in white, with bare shoulders as white as snow – the picture of youth, unprotected innocence, and humble virgin simplicity. "I must be very quiet," thought Rebecca, "and very interested about India."' (Chap. 3)

Thackeray addresses the reader at an early stage to point out that Becky is only doing for herself what most girls have mothers to do for them, thereby again involving his remarkable heroine in the typicality of the marriage-market, female display, drawing-room ballads and young ladies' painting. She is expressive of a general indictment. He also draws attention to the immaturity and relative incompetency of her performance. The first act as *ingénue* wanting a husband, fails, because of chance – rack-punch at Vauxhall – and because of George Osborne's snobbery. The first act is linked with a later one in which Becky enjoys both pure ridicule and revenge : when she later makes a play for George, it is in full recollection of his part in stopping her marriage to Jos. Moreover, Becky tries on two subsequent occasions to get Jos, and eventually of course succeeds.

As the novel develops, the reader is expected to read the behaviouristic mode without many incursions into Becky's mind, which also become unnecessary because she, as well as the reader, becomes more efficient. Sometimes the words alone show the performance, but Thackeray usually accompanies them with descriptions that stay markedly outside feeling and motive. He will describe language solely in terms of sound : 'accents of extreme delight', 'she dropped her voice', 'gave a great sigh', 'added, with a laugh', 'her deep-toned voice faltered' and so on. The impression is sharpened by a contrast between such dwelling on what is visible and audible in Becky, and what goes on inside other characters whose behaviour is less controlled and planned.

Becky's performances merge the highly professional acting and singing and dancing with her continuous personal performance, but of course that professionalism is relative. Thackeray makes this plain with one brilliantly complex stroke when he shows Becky's attitude to the professional artists engaged to entertain the great world. In Chapter 51, 'A Charade Is Acted', she discusses performance with Lord Steyne. The reader is unlikely to have forgotten the previous chapter, in which Amelia tried her hand at performance for profit – the painting of 'a couple of begilt Bristol boards' – but has had them rejected by the Fancy Repository and Brompton Emporium of Fine Arts. We have also heard of her writing to Jos, and in the phrase Thackeray uses to describe her letter, 'painting with artless pathos', the connection between her lack of art in human relations and in aesthetic effort is made clear. The connection between the use of art in human relations and aesthetic effort has already been made clear, by now, in the case of Becky. Chapter 51 makes one of many silent but strong contrasts between the two heroines.

Becky has entered the great world, the Babylon, the very inner circle of London fashion, and she has begun to perform, by singing to a little *comité* in a party given by the Prince of Peterwardin, with Lord Steyne 'paternally superintending the progress of his pupil'. On one occasion she tells Steyne about her ennui, in one of several confidential conversations that tell much about their relation : 'O how much gayer it would be to wear spangles and trousers, and dance before a booth at a fair.' She is using for effect an absolutely honest view which comes up again in Pumpernickel, when we see her resilience and adaptability in Bohemian society. She confides a genuine boredom, but the confiding is a performance : 'She used to tell the great man her *ennuis* and perplexities in her artless way – they amused him.' Becky is clever enough to use truth-telling artfully.

She stops talking because Pasta is beginning to sing, and Thackeray makes one of those awkward traps for the reader, first allowing us to enjoy chalking up a good mark for Becky, then suddenly making us erase it :

> Becky always made a point of being conspicuously polite to the professional ladies and gentlemen who attended at these aristocratic parties – of following them into the corners where they sate in silence, and shaking hands with them, and smiling in the view of all persons. She was an artist herself, as she said very truly : there was a frankness and humility in the manner in which she acknowledged her origin, which provoked, or disarmed, or amused lookers-on, as the case may be. (Chap. 51)

Her performance not only exploits and enjoys truth and candour, but it has a subtle impact. So has Thackeray's. While we are musing on the complexity of her act, Thackeray puts in a further twist by reminding us that while Becky enjoys embarrassing and reproaching the great world with her courtesy and honesty, she seldom does anything disinterestedly : 'Becky went her own way, and so fascinated the professional personages, that they would leave off their sore throats in order to sing at her parties and give her lessons for nothing.'

A little later she is ostentatiously talking French to a celebrated French tenor, and winning Lady Grizzel Macbeth by her performance of humility. Thackeray makes quite plain the continuity of the whole performance. He calls the episode where she is apparently most gratefully playing and singing to Lady Steyne (Chap. 49), 'the music scene'. In it Becky sings out of sincere gratitude, but the choice of music, 'religious songs of Mozart', is scarcely artless. Thackeray makes it plain that Becky needs all her arts in 'the great world', and that the great world, while demanding entertainment, is not good either at providing the arts, or at appreciating and detecting them. In the great charade evening, we are told that charades enable 'the many ladies amongst us who had beauty to display their charms, and the fewer number who had cleverness to exhibit their wit'. Becky plays Clytemnestra, allowing Steyne the witticism 'quite killing in her part' and the recognition that 'By —, she'd do it too'. That performance is followed by 'Mrs Rawdon Crawley in powder and patches, the most *ravissante* Little Marquise in the world'. She acts the innocent, as she does so frequently and effectively off the stage, singing the idyllic and cynical song[4] which stylizes and sophisticates pastoral,

'Thus each performs his part, Mamma, the birds have found
their voices
The blowing rose a flush, Mamma, her bonny cheek to dye.'

Becky's song, like her appearance, insists on cosmetic and performance.

Becky, however, has reached 'her culmination', as Thackeray insists. It is both appropriately ironic that she should only masquerade as a marquise, and that the heady praise may be what leads her into a very bad performance on the day after the party. But the novel shows her resilience, and at its end we see her once more acting the double role of Clytemnestra, and of the injured innocent. She may have killed Jos, but her last appearance is at a real 'fancy fair', not indeed in tights and spangles but in a more effective costume, considering the audience.

The characters of *Vanity Fair* are involved in performance in many ways, as actors and actresses, audience, manager, producer. There are a few people who do not act. Amelia is too sincere, mistaken, artless, Dobbin is utterly genuine. Miss Jemima and Briggs, both honest and rather dim, are presented by the author

[4] Only appearing cynical to the reader, of course, not to her audience within the novel.

without any analysis of the relationship of their goodness to their dimness. Thackeray takes care to criticize intelligence but he does not think that sincerity is enough. All the same, it is quite plainly superior to performance. It tends to be unprofitable : because Amelia cannot paint for profit, she has to hand over her child to the Osbornes, and because Dobbin cannot act, he lacks charm and plays second fiddle to George. George is not exactly a brilliant actor, being rather stupid, but he is a performer, in his way :

'There's not a finer fellow in the service,' Osborne said, 'nor a better officer, though he is not an Adonis, certainly.' And he looked towards the glass himself with much *naiveté*. (Chap. 5)

He walked up to Rebecca with a patronising, easy swagger. He was going to be kind to her and protect her. He would even shake hands with her, as a friend of Amelia's. . . . (Chap. 14)

He saw a slave before him in that simple yielding faithful creature, and his soul within him thrilled secretly somehow at the knowledge of his power. He would be generous-minded, Sultan as he was, and raise up this kneeling Esther and make a queen of her. . . . (Chap. 20)

His pulse was throbbing and his cheeks flushed : the great game of war was going to be played, and he one of the players. . . . What were all the games of chance he had ever played compared to this one? Into all contests requiring athletic skill and courage, the young man, from his boyhood upwards, had flung himself with all his might. The champion of his school and his regiment, the bravos of his companions had followed him everywhere; from the boys' cricket-match to the garrison-races, he had won a hundred of triumphs; and wherever he went, women and men had admired and envied him. (Chap. 30)

Readers often seem to take him at Becky's estimate, 'that selfish humbug, that low-bred cockney dandy, that padded booby', but there are things in George that the reader sees and that Becky does not. His is a very interesting, almost involuntary performance, not coming, like Becky's, or Mrs Bute's, or Lord Steyne's, out of self-possession and skilful production, but out of the common kind of vanity that sees itself in self-approved and enviable roles. George is not a simple character. His passion for

gambling, for instance, blends with his English schoolboy love
of games, both joined and surpassed by the war game. Thackeray's psychology here admits that stupid people may perform as
well as clever ones, and insists that George's desire is not for
profit in the financial sense, but for the profits of admiration
and envy, which include those of military fame and glory.

Thackeray, then, shows performance as including the dramatic
sense, the desire to project, to win, and to be admired by an
audience within and without. It is the unintelligent George,
rather than the self-possessed Becky, who displays the insidious
and common performance of our own passions. Out of the other
heroines, Beatrix, Blanche Amory and Ethel Newcome, not one
is a performer like Becky. Beatrix and Ethel, for all their differences in sensibility and total response, are both shown as seduced
into performance by the way of the great world, partly despising
it, partly enjoying it. Neither acts in cold-blooded appraisal and
plan, like Becky, but each has some interest in profit. Beatrix
wants rank, and her sexual career in *Esmond* is one of a steady
ambitious climb. Ethel is more complaisant, and also, when it
comes to the point, more proud, but her pride comes at the end
of real, if ambivalent, acquiescence in family aspiration. Thackeray shows in them both the desire for the performer's rewards,
applause and admiration. What appears faintly in George's
vanity and ambition, and in his enjoyment of praise, is fully
developed in all the heroines. On the night of the great charades,
when Becky's performances as singer and actress are most professional, even she is involved in that reckless self-love that comes
when strong applause goes to the head. It is this delight in social
rather than sexual ambition that Thackeray emphasizes in Becky
– interestingly, there is always great self-possession when she is
with men, Jos, Rawdon, Sir Pitt, George, Steyne, Loder. She is
the kind of utterly self-controlled courtesan who feigns passion
rather than feels it; her sense of triumph is concerned with the
reception of performance and social success, while Beatrix and
Ethel share a warmer, animal delight in body, looks and vitality.
Their vitality is closer to George's enjoyment of the games of
cards, sport and war. But they are certainly concerned with
profit, and the marriage-market is of course one of Thackeray's
chief social targets, shown over and over again in imagery of
Eastern harems and sirens. Most of his heroines enjoy being

sirens, at least up to a point. There is one rather nasty siren-illustration in *Lovel the Widower* (in The Harry Furniss Centenary Edition, 1911) where some hefty mother-sirens push their more seductive daughters towards the surface. The mother-sirens are always behind the performances, except in the case of Becky, who is alone, and Beatrix, whose mother loathes the game and its object. The most pathetic siren is probably Rosey, who is described almost entirely in behaviouristic terms, like Becky, so that she can emerge simply as a hollow puppet; she is continually described as little, charming and complaisant, but the chief source of our feeling that she is hollow comes from Thackeray's total refusal ever to show her from the inside. What she rather frighteningly lacks is the vitality of the other sirens. The siren is an image which links performance (the sirens sang for profit) with sexual seductiveness. Thackeray is good at conveying the origins of seductive performance with a 'natural' pleasure in looks and vitality. The act is a half-sincere one: the characters project themselves in flattering roles, but the roles are partly theirs by nature and nurture, involving a common and healthy enjoyment of youth and physicality. Ethel is often shown as flushed and in high spirits, and Thackeray does not need to analyse or separate the vitality which charmed others from her own pleasure in it: nothing succeeds like sexual success, and when Ethel is seen at the height of a ball, or a season, she is said to be 'in perfectly stunning spirits'. At times, Ethel's enjoyment is mixed with bravado, as in the ball at Baden, when she performs the part of belle of the ball, with recklessness and a mixture of self-contempt and social contempt which brings her close to Dickens's dark heroines. But she is quite unlike Ethel Dombey and Estella, because she does act partly for pleasure:

> Ethel kept the ball alive by herself almost. . . . Miss Ethel conducted herself as a most reckless and intrepid young flirt, using her eyes with the most consummate effect, chattering with astounding gaiety, prodigal of smiles, gracious thanks, and killing glances. (Chap. 33)

She is compared with an actress of 'the Varietés going to a supper at the Trois Frères', and here she is seen in her star performance, undertaken to spite the great world, herself, her

THE MOTHER SYRENS

grandmother and Madame d'Ivry, who has been Lord Kew's mistress. She is beating them all at their own game, and going beyond her part, that of the beautiful but not too conspicuous *ingénue*.

Later in the novel, after she has lost Lord Kew by this dazzling performance – an experiment conducted partly by the moral sense and partly by reckless jealousy, a die cast without foresight – Thackeray further explores her capacity for display and vivacity. Ethel does seem to become contaminated by the great world. The ball at Baden was a contemptuous and jealous performance, but it marks a change in Ethel, who has been too dignified, stately and forbidding for a popular success. Just as Thackeray shows Colonel Newcome as slightly tainted by being too much in the great world, so he shows Ethel stooping to the stupid and depraved Marquis of Farintosh, and participating more fervently in the great world :

She whirled round the dancing-room with him in triumph, the other beauties dwindling before her; she looked more and more beautiful with each rapid move of the waltz, her colour heightening and her eyes seeming to brighten. Not till the music stopped did she sink down on a seat, panting, and smiling radiant – as many, many hundred years ago I remember to have seen Taglioni, after a conquering *pas seul*. (Chap. 41)

On the same evening, Pendennis, as narrator, observes to Clive,

'Yes, she is a flirt. She can't help her nature. She tries to vanquish every one who comes near her. She is a little out of breath from waltzing, and so she pretends to be listening to poor Bustington, who is out of breath too, but puffs out his best in order to make himself agreeable. With what a pretty air she appears to listen! Her eyes actually seem to brighten.' (Ibid.)

Thackeray develops the idea of a half-involuntary participation in self-display and performance for the great world. In Ethel's case, it is presented most brilliantly by physical details like those in the last description : the enjoyment of the dance, the movement, the triumph, are convincingly and cunningly blended. Thackeray knew perfectly well that dramatic performance is not wholly an impersonation, and his heroines, like George Eliot's

Rosamond, can also 'act themselves'; sometimes, only a part of themselves. Ethel's vitality, beauty and capacity for enjoyment lend themselves to the profitable performance, but her judgment has to be suspended. Moreover, performance is not wholly within our control : one of the interesting suggestions made explicitly and implicitly in *The Newcomes* is that we act emotion until we cannot distinguish the act from genuine feeling. Thackeray does not explicitly reveal this insight through Ethel, but it seems to lie behind his leisurely presentation of her début, success and ultimate withdrawal from the great world. Her last interview with the Marquis of Farintosh explains that she has been acting, and intends to stop. The difficulty she has in explaining this to him is a tribute to her performance as well as to his stupidity.

Beatrix, in *Esmond*, is a different case, to be won by the great world. We first see her as a beautiful child, spoilt, it is suggested, by the great world and by her parents. In Chapter 11 Harry Esmond meets the grown Beatrix for the first time; she is naïve still, as blushes and tactless remarks about her father show, but she asks why Harry does 'not wear a peruke like my Lord Mohun?' Make-up, disguise, pretence make their entry. She also performs :

> Beatrix could sing and dance like a nymph. Her voice was her father's delight after dinner. She ruled over the house with little imperial ways, which her parents coaxed and laughed at. She had long learned the value of her bright eyes, and tried experiments in coquetry, *in corpore vili*, upon rustics and country squires, until she should prepare to conquer the world and the fashion. (Bk 1, Chap. 11)

In a novel about royalty, revolution and war, Thackeray often uses the imagery of conquest in describing Beatrix, whereas he more often uses the imagery of buying and selling in *The Newcomes* and *Vanity Fair* to describe the same sexual performance. It is a performance which she gradually improves, and by which she climbs, suitor by suitor, until the final conquest of the Pretender. But Beatrix is shown as noticeably less clever than Becky, Blanche or Ethel, and her acts are always less controlled and produced. Thackeray emphasizes her health, high spirits, exuberance and self-delight, and though she does from time to time experience ennui, it is not a bad case. She is the only heroine who is described amorously, by Esmond, remembering his love :

> Esmond had left a child and found a woman, grown beyond the common height; and arrived at such a dazzling completeness of beauty, that his eyes might well show surprise and delight at beholding her. In hers there was a brightness so lustrous and melting, that I have seen a whole assembly follow her as if by an attraction irresistible : and that night the great duke was at the playhouse after Ramillies, every soul turned and looked (she chanced to enter at the opposite side of the theatre at the same moment) at her, and not at him. She was a brown beauty : that is, her eyes, hair, and eyebrows and eyelashes, were dark : her hair curling with rich undulations, and waving over her shoulders; but her complexion was as dazzling white as snow in sunshine; except her cheeks, which were a bright red, and her lips, which were of a still deeper crimson. Her mouth and chin, they said, were too large and full, and so they might be for a goddess in marble, but not for a woman whose eyes were fire, whose look was love, whose voice was the sweetest low song, whose shape was perfect symmetry, health, decision, activity, whose foot as it planted itself on the ground, was firm but flexible, and whose motion, whether rapid or slow, was always perfect grace – agile as a nymph, lofty as a queen – now melting, now imperious, now sarcastic : there was no single movement of hers but was beautiful. As he thinks of her, he who writes feels young again, and remembers a paragon. (Bk 2, Chap. 7)

It is well known that *Esmond*, the novel described by Thackeray as a book of 'cut-throat melancholy', was written, as the author himself openly said,[5] at a time of extreme unhappiness, after he stopped seeing Jane Brookfield.[6] Although the story as such bears no resemblance to Thackeray's own love and loss, the feelings of deprivation, jealousy and unhappiness in marriage reflect his personal experience. It should also be said that it is

[5] *Letters*, Vol. III, p. 391.

[6] Jane Elton married William Brookfield, Thackeray's college friend, in March 1841, and Thackeray met her for the first time several months later, at about the same time as his wife entered a mental hospital. But it was not until 1846-7, when the Brookfields' marriage ran into difficulties, that Thackeray and Jane Brookfield began that exchange of confidences and affection that William Brookfield forcibly ended in September 1851.

Thackeray's only amorous novel : if his miseries coloured *Henry Esmond*, so too did his desires. In *Vanity Fair*, the only real portraiture of desire, in Lord Steyne, is unmistakably hostile, but into the portrait of Beatrix, admittedly eighteenth-century in style and content, goes a more than antiquarian feeling. Her vitality has a special glow for being presented, dramatically, from the viewpoint of the lover : 'shining eyes smile' upon Esmond, who 'could look at nothing but her eyes'; 'with the brightest eyes and sweetest smile'; 'Love seemed to radiate from her'; 'Harry eyed her with such a rapture as the first lover is described as having by Milton'. Beatrix is described lavishly, richly and brilliantly, with an emphasis on colour, movement, lustre, even details of clothing, and the method, with its effect, is unlike anything else in Thackeray. The presentation is not only sensual, but tenderly reminiscent. We are often made aware that the rapture is recollected in nostalgia, for though the novel contains the climactic moment when his love drops from him, the beginning has made it plain that the love is also permanently enshrined, 'there was never one so beautiful as that one'.

All the more distressing, then, when the beauty is used to captivate and climb : 'Such a pair of bright eyes as hers learn their power very soon.' Sexual beauty is equated with jewels, reduced to an object, a marketable object, and a dangerously valuable yet trivial one :

> I have looked at royal diamonds in the jewel-rooms in Europe, and thought how wars have been made about 'em . . . daring lives lost in digging out the little shining toys that I value no more than the button in my hat. And so there are other glittering baubles (of rare water too) for which men have been set to kill and quarrel ever since mankind began; and which last but for a score of years, when their sparkle is over. Where are those jewels now that beamed under Cleopatra's forehead, or shone in the sockets of Helen? (Bk 2, Chap. 7)

This draws on bitterness, plainly, but it is more than Esmond's lament for a brief and dangerous beauty. It is also part of the insistent presentation of Beatrix as a valuable object, ironical and critical, showing her less as a great performer in coquetry (though she is that) than marvellous and dazzling. Brilliance, shine and dazzle are linked with her as frequently as whiteness and freshness for Becky. Such imagery functions partly to show Esmond's obsessed desire, and to project Beatrix's image as something expensive, a commodity of high price. The imagery of richness, jewels, gold, silver and fine clothes relates to rank as well as price :

> There was a certain charm about this girl of which neither Colonel Esmond nor his fond mistress could forego the fascination; in spite of her faults and her pride and wilfulness, they were forced to love her; and, indeed, might be set down as the two chief flatterers of the brilliant creature's court. (Bk 3, Chap. 6)

Suggestions of rank join with suggestions of valuable things, to present Beatrix in terms less of an act than a display of charm and charms. Both Beatrix and Ethel, different though they are, show Thackeray merging nature and art in an insistence that natural beauty and sexual vitality are useful in the performance for profit, and not only in the Vanity Fair of the England of Queen Anne.

Pendennis contains three very interesting women characters in whom nature and art appear simply, distinctly and separately. Ethel and Beatrix are a mixture, a contamination or exploitation of nature by an artful, acquisitive and ambitious society. Laura is totally without art, though she is not a fool. The Fotheringay is delightfully split, a perfect 'natural' actress, able to behave exactly as the producer tells her, and utterly without guile as she makes her 'poyes' and asks what all that talk was about Hamlet and Kotzebue. It was clever of Thackeray to choose as his great actress someone with no acting capacity at all off-stage, incapable of the necessary understanding and analysis for the life-performances, but possessed of all the negative capability that can obey, reflect and imitate in stage-projection. The third character, Blanche Amory, sentimental poet, singer, coquette and life-actress, represents an interesting psychological view of the possible consequences of performance.

Blanche performs, and Thackeray suggests that performance eventually gets a grip of her, so that she becomes a monstrous figure, not because she will sell herself to the highest bidder, like Becky or Beatrix, but because she becomes incapable of distinguishing between performance and reality. She is a more frightening figure than Beatrix, who projects a predominantly physical charm and sexuality, or Becky, who offers wit, entertainment and an appropriately diversified performance for a large audience. Beatrix says she has no heart, Becky never shows any sign of having one, and although Blanche shares their coldness and hardness, her performance is very different. Hers is a specialized performance of sensibility. Of all the nineteenth-century English novelists, Thackeray and Meredith strike me as the only two who approach Stendhal's insight in the chronicle of emotion, and in his portrait of Blanche, Thackeray may perhaps claim the title of a poor man's – or an Englishman's – Stendhal. However, he lacks Stendhal's sense that the 'normal' emotional life is unsteady, erratic, histrionic, even assumed, and shows the histrionic performance and projection as a sign of contamination. Pen is most genuine when he loves an actress, and learns most about acting when he flirts with Blanche. Their relationship elevates flirtation, a subject Thackeray is always interested in, from an amusing sexual game into a sensitive and instructive drama of the feelings. What Blanche and Pen show is that you cannot always draw the line between sincerity and acting, that people can move into a hideous world of shadow-feeling where there is no sincerity any more.

Blanche herself is depicted in very stylized terms, as exaggeratedly aesthetic in her colour harmony, a kind of grotesque, comic and satiric pre-parody of Whistler's White Girl. The parody is perhaps perfected and appropriately grossened, when the chef, Mirobolant, provides an appropriate meal for Blanche, as decorative and unreal as her poems, though as it happens a more genuine record and token of sensibility, one of the few love-feasts in Thackeray :

'I determined that my dinner should be as spotless as the snow. At her accustomed hour, and instead of the rude *gigot à l'eau*, which was ordinarily served at her too simple table, I sent her up a little *potage à la Reine* – *à la Reine Blanche* I called it – as white as her own tint – and confectioned with the most fragrant cream and almonds. I then offered up at her shrine a *filet de merlan à l'Agnès*, and a delicate *plat*, which I have designated as *Éperlan à la Sainte Thérèse*, and of which my charming miss partook with pleasure. I followed this by two little *entrées* of sweetbread and chicken; and the only brown thing which I permitted myself in the entertainment was a little roast of lamb, which I laid in a meadow of spinaches, surrounded with *croustillons*, representing sheep, and ornamented with daisies and other savage flowers. After this came my second service : a pudding *à la Reine Elizabeth* (who, Madame Fribsbi knows, was a maiden princess); a dish of opal-coloured plovers' eggs, which I called *Nid de tourtereaux à la Roucoule*; placing in the midst of them two of those tender volatiles, billing each other, and confectioned with butter; a basket containing little *gâteaux* of apricots, which, I know, all young ladies adore; and a jelly of marasquin, bland, insinuating, intoxicating as the glance of beauty. This I designated *Ambroisie de Calypso à la Souveraine de mon Coeur.*' (Chap. 23)

The effect is similar to the behaviouristic descriptions of Becky and Rosey, or the emphasis on the dazzling appearance of Beatrix, in reifying character. In this case the individual appears as a work of art, appropriately white, because white stands for good saleable purity, and because Blanche is colourless, humanly null. This effect is produced in her pride in blondeness, 'My name is Blanche – isn't it a pretty name? Call me by it' and '*je suis Blanche et blonde*'. She shares her fairness with Becky, also the telltale shade of green (in Blanche's case, in her hair, but still the sinister mermaid colour). She has something of Rosey's littleness and sweetness, and the illustration shows her face as unequivocally charming, without Becky's emblematic and unvaryingly forced and sinister smiling mouth. From her very first words to Laura, in Chapter 23, 'New Faces', she announces the theme of sensibility : 'I, too, have suffered', 'I already love you as a sister', 'It is electricity – spontaneity. It is instantaneous'. She is utterly self-absorbed, asking questions but not listening to answers, in love with her reflection in the glass. Her self-devotion is powerfully drawn, and her book of poems, *Mes Larmes*, manages to convey egocentricity, sensibility, poetic effusiveness, and an imported French affectation, all in two words. The combination of love and death is sweetened and diminished in this little decorative portrait : 'She was familiar with the idea of suicide. Death she repeatedly longed for. A faded rose inspired her with such grief that you would have thought she must die in pain of it.'

Thackeray uses her as an appropriate attachment for Pen,

whose poetic sensibility she stimulates and indeed parodies. He responds in poems, some of them twice-turned. But Blanche also appears like Becky in her ruthlessness and cruelty, indeed she goes beyond Becky in being unpleasantly sadistic, frightening, threatening and spiteful, living, as Thackeray sharply observes, 'like many a genius, with those who did not understand her'.

At first Thackeray merely shows the discrepancy between the appearance and the truth, stressing the sensitive, sentimental performance of the hard, cold little actress. This is the strain of Pen's early mock-pastoral idyll with Blanche, but it changes later on, when they renew their acquaintance and when Major Pendennis begins to plan a *mariage de convenance* for the two sentimentalists. Thackeray first shows Pen responding to Blanche as one sentimental poet to another. One of his themes is Pen's artistic growth as a realistic novelist like Thackeray. (In *The Newcomes* there is one episode where Ethel sternly asks Pendennis, matured into a spectator, friend and narrator, why he doesn't introduce good women, just as some of Thackeray's critics accused him of unrelieved cynicism.) Thackeray is also interested in showing the artistic temperament's susceptibility to 'twaddle',[7] especially when decorative and sweet; and he is even

[7] A word he uses with care, ironically in the mouth of Jones, in Chapter 1 of *Vanity Fair*, and when he writes to say that Mrs Proctor will be glad that he has sent Colonel Newcome back to India and suggests that she finds the Colonel a 'twaddler'. (*Letters*, Vol. III, p. 341)

more interested in showing how an intelligent man can compromise with the world, with his eyes open. The young Pen plays
poets with Blanche to pass the time, and the slightly more mature
Pen is still willing to trifle sweetly with her and to play the
Major's game. But Blanche still wants the graces of poetry and
sentiment, while Pen, for his part, wants something in its way
equally self-indulgent, the luxury of candour. Thackeray, so
often accused of being a cynic, shows how far removed he is
from cynicism by dramatizing the cynic in Pen, in many ways the
character nearest to Thackeray, in career, some aspects of life,
and in the progress of his art.

Blanche too accuses Pen of cynicism (Chap. 64), calls him
'monsieur le misantrope', and bitterly resents his rejection of
their pastoral game : 'Is your Psyche an odious vulgar wretch?
You wicked satirical creature, I can't abide you !' This time she
really cries, and doesn't like it, 'You – you make me cry, that
you do.' Arthur, just as selfish, refuses to play, though his reasons
are neither very intelligent nor very creditable, and he is posturing as the disillusioned lover : 'I don't think I have much of
what people call heart; but I don't profess it. I made my venture
when I was eighteen, and lighted my lamp and went in search
of Cupid. And what was my discovery of love ! – a vulgar
dancing woman.' When he tells Blanche he will not flatter her,
will not repeat their childish game of verses, or feed her with
bon-bons, she tries to continue the sweet childish role, with *'Mais
j'adore les bonbons, moi'*, but with 'a queer piteous look', that
becomes 'genuine tears of vexation', which he tries to console. One
of her best moments comes when she refuses to take a consoling
kiss after he has refused to make love sentimentally. This rather
dignified response is immediately followed by one of Thackeray's
sensitive psychological observations, reminiscent of Becky's admiration of Rawdon in the discovery scene :

> The scornful and sarcastic tone of Pendennis quite frightened
> and overcame the girl. 'I – I don't want your consolation. I – I
> never was – so – spoken to bef – by any of my – my – by –
> anybody' – she sobbed out, with much simplicity.
> *'Anybody!'* shouted out Pen, with a savage burst of laughter,
> and Blanche blushed one of the most genuine blushes which her
> cheek had ever exhibited, and she cried out, 'O, Arthur, *vous
> êtes un homme terrible !*' (Chap. 64)

Pen laughs because her *ingénue* act has collapsed before his
blasé one, and it is plain that she has no right to object to his
refusal to be sentimental. Thackeray shows her emotional response as a loss of control, as confusion, and as some real
feeling : 'She felt bewildered, frightened, oppressed, the worldly
little flirt who had been playing at love for the last dozen years
of her life, and yet not displeased at meeting a master.' (Ibid.)
'Master' is ambiguous. Pen has mastered her by playing the
game on his terms, and thus ruining her act, disconcerting her
and giving her the pleasure of defeat, experiences peculiarly
enjoyable to one so contained by rules and routines and therefore so vulnerable to ennui. He is also a master in another sense,
as a performer, for all the cynicism is disingenuous, since he has
not chosen to question the schemes of his uncle, and replies to
her questions about Sir Francis 'with a forced laugh'. He sends
her the bon-bons after all, with verses both ready-made and 'of
his own manufacture, quite as artless and authentic', and
Thackeray's last paragraph makes it difficult to prefer Pendennis
to Blanche : 'at least the renegade did not pretend to be a
believer in the creed to which he was ready to swear'. Thackeray
then turns another corner, in a generalization which involves the
reader and the writer :

> And if every woman and man in this kingdom, who has sold her
> or himself for money or position, as Mr Pendennis was about to
> do, would but purchase a copy of his memoirs, what tons of
> volumes Messrs Bradbury and Evans would sell ! (Ibid.)

The author insists on his own profitable performance, as he
criticizes the profitable performance of his characters.

In the end, Pen does not sell himself, and is saved. Blanche's
performance, however, grows and matures. Pen discovers the
plot, gives up his uncle and the world, is persuaded by Laura
that he must stick to the game with Blanche, and offers her
himself and the drama of real life, in appropriate and moving
images of roles, fictions and dreams of sacrifice :

> 'Dear Blanche,' Arthur wrote, 'you are always reading and
> dreaming pretty dramas, and exciting romances in real life, are

you now prepared to enact a part of one? And not the pleasantest part, dear Blanche, that in which the heroine takes possession of her father's palace and wealth, and introducing her husband to the loyal retainers and faithful vassals, greets her happy bridegroom with "All of this is mine and thine", – but the other character, that of the luckless lady . . . that of Alnaschar's wife. . . .' (Chap. 72)

It is a good letter, from one artist to another, but from Pen's more sensitive self-indulgence and more honest honesty, to a Blanche he knows well. Her reply is also rather good, showing how the language of sensibility can be used evasively to avoid concreteness and commitment: 'To you I bring the gushing poesy of my being – the yearnings of the soul that longs to be loved – that pines for love, love, love, beyond, all! – that flings itself at your feet, and cries, Love, me, Arthur!' (Ibid.)

We have seen them as 'two battered London rakes', playing at love, and we have seen Blanche confused and moved by Pen's refusal to play the sentimental game. Now we see how his honest proposal is answered by a sentimental retreat. In a way, her reply, for all its gushing vagueness, is clever and practical, since it allows her to play for time. Pen cannot read the letter, and remarks on 'his slippery fortune', turning over 'the musky gilt-edged riddle. It amused his humour: he enjoyed it as if it had been a funny story'.

In the discovery scene where Pen finds his 'little Syren' singing 'with all her might and fascinations' to Foker, with a serpentine diamond bracelet[8] in its purple-leather box, there is the last stage of this sentimental analysis. Pen allows Blanche her act before Foker, then when they are alone, urges her to tell him the truth about her father (the guilty secret in the novel, not handled very well by Thackeray, but serving its purpose in precipitating such passions and performances). She, for her part, says he has never loved her, and explains herself with some insight:

'*Et moi c'est different.* I have been spoilt early. I cannot live out of the world, out of excitement. I could have done so, but it is too late. If I cannot have emotions, I must have the world. You would offer me neither one nor the other.' (Chap. 73)

[8] In the discovery scene in *Vanity Fair*, Becky is similarly associated with the Fall, her hands being 'covered with serpents, and rings, and baubles'.

Which is true enough. He seems to hark back to the earlier scene where she felt something, if only confused respect, in the implication of her preference for '*un homme qui fera parler de moi?*'

Then she suddenly turns to another emotion, after we had thought that she was appealing to Pen :

'*Je l'aime, mon pauvre père, voyez-vous?* I would rather live with that man than with you *fades* intriguers of the world. I must have emotions – *il m'en donne. Il m'écrit. Il écrit très-bien, voyez-vous – comme un pirate – comme un Bohémien – comme un homme.* But for this I would have said to my mother – *Ma mère! quittons ce lâche mari, cette lâche société – retournons à mon père.*' (Ibid.)

Thackeray's handling of this final dialogue is masterly. Blanche's French takes over more and more, until the English phrases are what look like the quotations – like Becky, she uses French affectedly, but, unlike Becky, displays the special decorum in using it for the affectation of sensibility. Her language becomes almost feverish posturings. Pen seems to see her as a creature of transient feelings, too susceptible to ennui, for he says : 'The pirate would have wearied you like the rest.' Thackeray, having surprised Pen and the reader by Blanche's self-diagnosis, tells us that the truth is worse than Pen thinks. Pen feels that he has never known her until now, presumably responding to the savage candour of her disclosure and rejection in '*cette lâche société*'. But Thackeray rounds another corner :

Pen had never seen her or known so much about her in all the years of their intimacy as he saw and knew now : though he saw more than existed in reality. For this young lady was not able to carry out any emotion to the full; but had a sham enthusiasm, a sham hatred, a sham love, a sham taste, a sham grief, each of which flared and shone very vehemently for an instant, but subsided and gave place to the next sham emotion. (Ibid.)

In other words, Pen takes her too seriously. The omniscient author makes the hideous disclosure that she was not simply unable to have lasting emotions, but was unable to have any real ones. The act has become everything. It is not quite the last word, though, because Blanche is to lose Foker, to show how little this matters, and to make her exit on one last performance of sham feeling. She feels relief at losing her betrothed, and in histrionic language, 'Stay, mamma, stay' and a gesture 'which was always appropriate, though rather theatrical', she makes the last offer, 'to keep the secret of my mother's shame', 'give up my rights' and in order – fine stroke – to prove 'heart'. We last hear of her in Paris, married, socially successful, and an author – 'Bungay bought her poems, and published them, with the countess's coronet emblazoned on the countess's work'. Thackeray's last reminder, after he has stripped layer from layer of affectation and performance, is that hollow men make successful poets, and that it always helps to have a coronet on the cover.

CHAPTER FOUR

The Expressive Things

The quasi-peaceable gentleman of leisure, then, not only consumes of the staff of life beyond the minimum required for subsistence and physical efficiency, but his consumption also undergoes a specialization as regards the quality of the goods consumed. He consumes freely and of the best, in food, drink, narcotics, shelter, services, ornaments, apparel, weapons and accoutrements, amusements, amulets, and idols or divinities.

Thorstein Veblen, *The Theory of the Leisure Class* (London, 1925), Chap. 4

'There is no such thing as an isolated man or woman; we are each of us made up of a cluster of appurtenances. What do you call one's self? Where does it begin? where does it end? It overflows into everything that belongs to us – and then it flows back again. I know that a large part of myself is in the dresses I choose to wear. I have a great respect for *things*! One's self – for other people – is one's expression of one's self; and one's house, one's clothes, the book one reads, the company one keeps – these things are all expressive.'

The Portrait of a Lady, Chap. 19

Therefore at this Fair are all such merchandise sold, as houses, lands, trades, places, honours, preferments, titles, countries, kingdoms, lusts, pleasures, and delights of all sorts, as whores, bawds, wives, husbands, children, masters, servants, lives, blood, bodies, souls, silver, gold, pearls, precious stones, and what not.

The Pilgrim's Progress

Unlike Christian and Faithful, who angered the merchants of the fair by setting 'very light by all their wares', Thackeray was attached to the things of this world. Food, drink, books, prints, furniture, clothes, presents, purchases are vivid in his biography. At his funeral, Millais recorded the presence of a 'crowd of women . . . dressed in all colours . . . [whose] scarlet and blue

95

feathers stood out'. I add to this most moving vanity, others recalled at random : the silver statuette of Punch, a present from admirers; the Georgian window over the marble fireplace in Palace Green, over which a mirror wound at night; the wax taper in a silver candlestick that he liked to take to bed; the 'mahogany tree'; the bin of port at a Gray's Inn coffee-house; a certain brown hock; carpets, cigars, tripe, canvas-back ducks; a silk-lined padded coat he wanted to buy for his stepfather when he was doing so well on his first American tour; the huge oysters that made him feel as if he had swallowed a baby. These and many other objects stand out as records of generosity, love, appreciation, enjoyment, good taste, sensuousness and prosperity. Then there are the memorable words of appreciation like '*high* living and high *thinking*' or the confession that he liked 'second-rate books, second-rate women, but first-rate wines'. In his life and his letters, things are appreciated and loved.

Fetishes and Idols

In his Vanity Fair, however, the environment of all his major novels, the things are suspect. Like Beatrix's eyes, human attributes tend to become commodities in a society which buys and sells a list of objects and people like Bunyan's. Bunyan's miscellany needs no change at all to become precisely descriptive of the things of Thackeray's fair. It is a fair which tends to turn people and human relations into merchandise, to reify and commercialize what ought to be personal and unpurchasable. Perhaps the most blatant sign of human commodities is Ethel Newcome's green ticket, a significant object which should be seen in its context. Ethel pins the ticket on herself to announce that she is for sale, inspired by seeing the 'sold' ticket on a painting :

> They came to a piece by Mr Hunt, representing one of those figures which he knows how to paint with such consummate truth and pathos – a friendless young girl, cowering in a door-way, evidently without home or shelter. The exquisite fidelity of the details, and the plaintive beauty of the expression of the child, attracted old Lady Kew's admiration, who was an excellent judge of works of art. . . . (Chap. 28)

It is plain that Lady Kew has aesthetic sensibility, 'could delight in pictures, applaud good poetry, and squeeze out a tear over a good novel too'. Thackeray makes Ethel take the ticket for herself, but only after she has apparently meditated on her grandmother's capacity to respond to in the work of art what she has no sympathy for in life. When Ethel wears the ticket it is not simply to declare that she is sold, it is also to declare herself to be No. 46 in the *tableau-vivant*, reduced to an object, just as nature – pathetic female nature – is reduced for appreciation and profit in the picture by Hunt. But very soon, on the next page, Thackeray shows Ethel as having an excessive appreciation of objects, and we see the connection between the old lady's human response to a painting, and her granddaughter's preference for things: 'Clive was but a fancy, if he had ever been so much as that, not a passion, and she fancied a pretty four-pronged coronet even more.' Lady Kew's earlier estimate of Ethel proves shrewd: ' . . . you belong to your belongings, my dear, and are not better than the rest of the world. . . .' The family resemblance declares itself; and, more important, declares the corruption of Vanity Fair.

Beatrix's eyes are compared with baubles, toys and jewels, in brightness, beauty and purchasing-power, and she is nearly always described in terms of her surrounding objects. All her vitality seems to reside in what Madame Merle, in *The Portrait of a Lady*, calls 'the shell', 'the whole envelope of circumstances', and the 'cluster of appurtenances': 'one's house, one's clothes, the book one reads, the company one keeps – these things are all expressive'. Henry James makes Isabel Archer reply that she feels the environment of things as a 'limit, a barrier', but the course of the novel shows that she is not able to retain her self intact and free of the cluster. Thackeray's novels show people who are almost completely expressed by their envelope of things, and even those who are free spirits often respond to the objects surrounding other people. Esmond, for instance, relates to Beatrix very plainly, through her expressive objects. Since this is a novel of memory, Thackeray often makes Esmond distinguish clearly between a past obsession and a present nostalgia. But both moods or states of feeling are largely presented through Beatrix's appearance, which is very dependent on objects. She

D

is, for example, described as illuminated by a wax candle, with the brilliant white of her neck set off by a scarlet ribbon; Esmond observes her red stockings with silver clocks, her white shoes, and, next day, grey stockings and black shoes. He feels her 'soft perfumed hair'. And in the same scene (Bk 2, Chap. 7), we may notice that he is wearing unusual finery. She had once asked him why he didn't wear a peruke like Lord Mohun, and Frank notices that he is looking 'fine' in 'scarlet and silver' with a black periwig. When he decides to take Rachel's advice and go away we hear that Beatrix 'had brought out a new gown and blue stockings'. As I have argued, costume is part of performance, especially for Becky, Blanche and Beatrix. It is also something much more : it is an aspect of an environment in which objects are aids to human response, stimulate it, and form signs and symbols in a sexual conversation. Esmond's response to Beatrix is seen, positively and negatively, in such details of clothing : he puts on colours to please and to answer and to signal. When he asks her if she has 'orders for the army', she asks for Mechlin lace. When Beatrix and Rachel perform the mock-ceremony of knighting Esmond, the daughter gives the ribbon, her mother the sword. Lord Ashburnham conducts his courtship of Beatrix 'in a new suit every week . . . decked out in all the finery that his tailor or embroiderer could furnish for him'. In the next chapter (Bk 3, Chap. 1), Thackeray puns as he observes that Esmond 'had no suit to play but the red one'. Beatrix nearly always thinks in terms of clothes : she dislikes parsons 'whether they wear cassocks and buckles, or beards and bare feet', says she can't be a Quaker because the dress is not becoming, compares a woman to a priest by calling a priest 'a robe', and thinks of Frank turned papist, 'with a white sheet and a candle walking in a procession barefoot'. It is at the end of this flight of sartorial imagination (Bk 3, Chap. 2) that she starts to mime the barefoot Frank and kicks off 'her little slippers (the wonderfullest little shoes with wonderful tall red heels . . .)' in a gesture which Esmond finds exciting. He pounces on the slipper, joins in her anti-papist mime by kissing her stockinged foot, and so arouses the jealous movement of Rachel's feet, 'quite as pretty' as her daughter's, with shoes made 'off the same last'. When Rachel rebukes Beatrix for jesting with sacred things – she jokes about worshipping images – she 'orders' her ribbons and adjusts her tucker. Her sacred things are finery, and desire makes them sacred for Esmond too. Rachel's tapping feet respond in sensitive jealousy, as well they may.

This fetishism does two things in *Esmond* : it shows Beatrix's worldliness, and it shows Esmond's sexual response and participation. Sex is a response to the social dress, as well as to the woman. Esmond compares his passion with other forms of obsession, that of a sovereign who gives half a kingdom for 'a little crystal as big as a pigeon's egg', a nobleman 'caballing for a blue ribbon' or a Dutch merchant paying ten thousand crowns for a tulip. But the irony of the comparisons lies not so much in the difference of the obsessions, all rendered conspicuously in terms of objects, as in their similarity. Esmond's is a desire for the surface, for the beauty, for the vanity. That is why he is able to lose it so abruptly at the end, though it has been so strong and genuine that he does not devalue it in the memory, but rather recollects the vanity, in tranquillity, to love it again. Thackeray wants to show his hero coming to his senses, but never forgetting what losing them was like :

Who, in the course of his life, hath not been so bewitched, and worshipped some idol or another? Years after this passion hath been dead and buried, along with a thousand other worldly cares and ambitions, he who felt it can recall it out of its grave, and admire, almost as fondly as he did in his youth, that lovely queenly creature. I invoke that beautiful spirit from the shades and love her still; or rather I should say such a past is always present to a man; such a passion once felt forms a part of his whole being, and cannot be separated from it. . . . (Bk 3, Chap. 6)

The idolatry is shown in this infatuation with the outside, with dress and decoration. And through the glamour and flaunted sexuality of the outside we see the strong desire, the hollow vanity and the social pressures.

But fetishism and idolatry take other forms in the novels of Thackeray. The theme of idolatry is very closely bound up with the theme of vanity, both being powerfully present in Thackeray's source books – *The Pilgrim's Progress* and the Old Testament.[1]

[1] In Daniel and Ecclesiastes.

Christian and Faithful are arrested and tried for a failure to worship the false icons, the things of Vanity Fair:

> . . . That which did not a little amuse the merchandisers was that these pilgrims set very light by all their wares, they cared not so much to look upon them; and if they called upon them to buy, they would put their fingers in their ears, and cry, *Turn away mine eyes from beholding vanity*; and look upwards, signifying that their trade and traffic was in Heaven. (*The Pilgrim's Progress*, Pt 1)

There are two noble women characters, Helen and Laura Pendennis – not Rachel, as we have seen from her jealous feet – who have their trade and traffic in Heaven, but most of Thackeray's characters are implicated in idolatry, one way or another. The ways differ quite a lot. Esmond is fully aware of the vanity and worldliness corrupting Beatrix, though he participates in the vanity, and even responds to it sensually and socially, valuing rank, success and money as means to the sensual end. In *Vanity Fair* nearly all the characters worship the false god of gold, silver, rank. Some trade, as Bunyan says, in 'wives, husbands, children': Becky marries Rawdon because he is Miss Crawley's heir, presents him as a 'bully',[2] deceives him, all for profit, she uses her child, exploits him and maternal love; Osborn tries to sell his son to Miss Swartz. 'Masters, servants': Becky robs and exploits her servants, some of whom own her house and supply her with food, and some of them are not surprisingly willing to make money or steal from her; Joseph Sedley and Isidore exploit each other in a relationship which is highly commercialized. 'Lives, blood, bodies': at Waterloo, and in all branches of the sexual market. 'Silver, gold, pearls, precious stones, and what not': Becky's diamonds, brocade and old lace, the Osbornes' presents to George, Lady Bareacres' jewels and so on.

There is the less obvious trade too. Two important characters in *Vanity Fair* who are not personally involved in acquisitiveness and commerce are Dobbin and Amelia. Dobbin's father was a grocer, and trade gave him an education as well as the nickname 'Figs'. Amelia's father is a stockbroker and his money gives her a comfortable start in life, her friendships, education, home and

[2] That is, pimp.

betrothal. War comes, and the funds fall. Amelia has to face poverty, becomes estranged from her mother and father, by meanness, anxiety, and quarrels over money and things.[3] Despite Amelia's losses from trade, despite the need to sacrifice and sell George to his grandfather, who certainly buys him with real money, she stands apart from the mercantile values. She does not sell her child because she wants the money but because she wants a decent life for him.[4] But she does make false gods out of her dead husband and her living son. Thackeray makes the idolatry plain by using an object, or rather by making Amelia use objects. She has icons and a shrine :

> . . . She looked up at George's picture, which hung there as usual, with the portrait of the boy underneath. ' . . . you were pure, my saint in heaven !'
> . . . She went and leaned on the chest of drawers over which the picture hung, and gazed and gazed at it. Its eyes seemed to look down on her with a reproach that deepened as she looked. The early dear memories of that brief prime of love rushed back upon her. (Chap. 66)

There is an interesting difference between Thackeray's criticisms of Amelia's idolatry and his tolerance of Esmond's. Esmond tells his story from within, and with very little self-criticism. One advantage of this first person memoir of idolatry is perhaps its unobtrusive insulation from criticism. Thackeray sees that worship of the child is common in women, but he is critical as well as sympathetic. He insists fiercely on the weak selfishness of Amelia's worship of her husband, an idolatry helped by the sifting of memory, and its sentimentalizing nostalgia for the good parts of the past. Dobbin attacks her for letting the 'abstract pathos' of her worship of George stand between her and a truly generous love. The idolatry stops, apparently because she has come to value a live Dobbin more than a dead George, and cannot go on having both. It has always been a shrine with two saints : she begins by worshipping her newly born child, and

---

[3] George Eliot and Thackeray followed Jane Austen in showing the debasing effect of poverty, especially for those who had seen better times.

[4] She is wrong about getting it by letting him go to the Osborne house, where he stands a good chance of being ruined like his father, but he is rescued in time, by death, chance, Dobbin's return.

the worship of the dead George then develops, the similarity of the eyes and identity of the name making the two idols reinforce each other. The pictures above the bed are the objects – not described – that make the idolatry plain; this is a form of prayer to an appearance, and the appearance is, like all pictures, a selection and an abstraction from real persons and real values.

In passing, Thackeray briefly implicates even Dobbin, who stops worshipping his false saint, Amelia, and replaces her with his daughter. There is the one brief word that tells us how incorrigible idolatry is, and especially the vain love of children by parents: ' . . . he was deeply immersed in his "History of the Punjaub", which still occupies him, and much alarmed about his little daughter, whom he idolizes. . . .' (Chap. 67)

Relics and Presents

Becky is contrasted with Amelia in so many ways, as schoolgirl, débutante, wife, mother, poor woman, rich woman, woman in time of war, and so on, that it is appropriate that she should have her false icon. As she has no heart, it is a parody, a doubly false relic, picked up long ago, in the Sedleys' sale, partly out of amusement, partly as a cheap souvenir. It is the picture of fat Joseph on an elephant, which turns up unexpectedly but more conveniently in Pumpernickel. The half-guinea bid has given Becky her money's worth: 'At last the much-bragged-about boxes arrived from Leipzig – three of them, not by any means large or splendid; – nor did Becky appear to take out any sort of dresses or ornaments from the boxes when they did arrive.' (Chap. 67)

The absence of dresses and ornaments is interesting. She has used them in the past, her cluster of appurtenances containing changes of clothing, some clean, some dirty, and a mask. It is not only with finery that she composes her drama, but with carefully chosen objects, properties to be kept and used at the right time on the right person:

But out of one . . . she took a picture with great glee, which she pinned up in her room, and to which she introduced Jos. It was the portrait of a gentleman in pencil, his face having the advantage of being painted up in pink. He was riding on an elephant, away from some cocoa-nut [*sic*] trees, and a pagoda : it was an Eastern scene.

'God bless my soul, it is my portrait,' Jos cried out. It was he indeed, blooming in youth and beauty, in a nankeen jacket of the cut of 1804. It was the old picture that used to hang up in Russell Square.

'I bought it,' said Becky, in a voice trembling with emotion; 'I went to see if I could be of any use to my kind friends. I have never parted with that picture – I never will.' (Ibid.)

Of course Jos's vanity is taken in, by the evidence of the picture, and his youthful image in the nankeen jacket.

Becky poses as idolatrous on this one occasion, but her relations with objects are detached and cool. Objects express her artfulness and artifices, for she uses them as she uses people, and in order to use people. There is one exception to this, when she produces the *billet-doux* George put in her bouquet long ago (though she has hung on to it in case it should come in handy). She produces it to incriminate George and persuade Amelia that he was not a saint, but as it happens, the object's magic is ineffective; Amelia has already sent for Dobbin, Becky is not allowed to be that powerful. Becky uses and abuses objects from the very beginning of the novel, when we see her rejecting the dictionary, which is not the usual false, formal and cheap leaving present from Miss Pinkerton, but in this one instance a real present, given with Miss Jemima's generosity. Thereafter, Becky appears in an entirely predatory relation with objects, envying them, accepting them, showing them off, scrounging, and using them to please and to solicit. What she does with objects is precisely what she does with people. She acquires objects as she acquires husband, lovers, friends and admirers, in order to get money and position. She hoards them, as she tends to hoard people, being the kind of person who calls keeping in touch 'keeping up contacts'. She charms and solicits presents in the form of champagne, game, love-letters, money, diamonds. She steals husbands, servants, food, houses, furniture, clothes, fine old brocade. She uses the elephant picture and tries to use the love-letter as persuasive objects. In the same way, but more disgracefully, she uses some military relics from the Battle of Waterloo, which come into the category of objects that might be sacred, though not to

Becky. She tries to use them to substantiate a fiction and to buy
back the goodwill (and money) of Miss Crawley. Becky's objects
are never sacred, her icons are pretences, and when she comes
bearing gifts she is out to get something :

> In the box were a pair of French epaulets, a Cross of the Legion
> of Honour, and the hilt of a sword – relics from the field of
> battle : and the letter described with a good deal of humour
> how the latter belonged to a commanding-officer of the Guard,
> who having sworn that 'the Guard died but never surrendered',
> was taken prisoner the next minute by a private soldier, who
> broke the Frenchman's sword with the butt of his musket, when
> Rawdon made himself master of the shattered weapon. As for
> the cross and epaulets they came from a Colonel of French
> cavalry, who had fallen under the aide-de-camp's arm in the
> battle : and Rawdon Crawley did not know what better to do
> with the spoils than to send them to his kindest and most
> affectionate old friend. (Chap. 33)

Becky is of course only one of many legacy-hunters; Mrs
Crawley, like Volpone, does well out of her predatory presents.
But there is something shamefully abusive in Becky's lies, which
reduce these anonymous relics of war to stage-properties and
fictions. When Thackeray describes how 'it was not only Becky
who wrote the letters, but . . . Mrs Rawdon actually took and
sent home the trophies – which she bought for a few francs, from
one of the innumerable pedlars who immediately began to deal
in relics of the war', he is very close to Bunyan. Becky is not only
getting something cheap, as she often does, but is perfectly put
in her place as one of 'the innumerable pedlars of the war' – also
of Vanity Fair, where innumerable pedlars buy and sell anything
that comes their way.

Becky's rise is marked by a certain sustained drama of present-
giving. Besides Johnson's dictionary, the statuary farewell
presentation, Amelia is also given a token of love, that bowpot
'as big as a haystack'. When Becky is staying with the Sedleys,
Jos brings bouquets for both the girls. In the Brussels Opera
House, George asks, 'Emmy, why didn't you have a bouquet?
Everybody has a bouquet.' 'Faith, then, why didn't you *boy*
one?' Mrs O'Dowd said. On the occasion of the great ball in
Brussels, her success and Amelia's failure is marked in another

bouquet-scene : Becky has the bouquet, Amelia has none. She even has to look after Becky's bouquet : ' . . . she left her bouquet and shawl by Amelia's side, and tripped off with George to dance'. Later, George goes off to give Becky the bouquet, 'but when he gave it to the owner, there lay a note, coiled like a snake among the flowers'. And Thackeray observes that Amelia saw 'part at least of the bouquet-scene'.

The bouquet motif continues, not merely in the preservation of the hidden letter, but in Becky's cool caring for the flowers after the ball, and after her husband has gone off to Waterloo :

> . . . She divested herself of this pink raiment; in doing which a note fell out from her corsage, which she picked up with a smile, and locked into her dressing-box. And then she put her bouquet of the ball into a glass of water, and went to bed, and slept very comfortably. (Chap. 30)

The bouquet lasts : 'After the reception of the previous day, Rebecca did not dare to come near her dear Amelia. She clipped the bouquet which George had brought her, and gave fresh water to the flowers. . . .' (Chap. 32)

The flowers last in order to register her success, and to compensate for the bouquet she did not receive long ago. The deliberate care for the flowers registers her detachment : the bouquet is no sacred relic, means nothing to her. The neatly clipped flowers contrast with that scarlet sash which Amelia worships fetishistically, and hysterically. Presents are invitations, solicitations, status symbols, love-tokens, protestations, rewards and bribes. People in Thackeray occasionally give presents in order to express their personal tastes, occasionally to give the other person what will gratify him, frequently to get something much better back as a result, sometimes to rid themselves of an unwanted object, very occasionally to follow a polite ritual, sometimes to hurt, often to give something small instead of something big, very often indeed to gratify themselves by gratifying someone they love. Miss Jemima's rejected dictionary seems to be the only disinterested present in all Thackeray. Amelia gives Georgy the books for Christmas, in a way common to parents, to bestow love and receive gratitude. They are interesting presents, designed both to educate and to please, 'the "Parent's Assistant", and the

"Sandford and Merton" Georgy longed for', with the superscription, ' "George Osborne, a Christmas gift from his affectionate mother". The books are extant to this day, with the fair
delicate superscription'. Thackeray, great artist as he is, always
defeats the narrowness of category : here he goes beyond the
expression of role and character, to utilize objects in a traditional
nostalgic lament for enviable permanence. This same cruel
survival of objects once given with love is found in another
shrine, in George Osborne's room, shut up for ten years in love
and anger, and opened again for Georgy, revealing clothes,
papers, whips, and the various sad odds and ends, including 'The
Bible his mother had given him'.

When Mrs Sedley's mother's eye is caught by 'the gilt bindings
of the seven handsome little volumes', she accuses Amelia of
buying books when she has had to sell 'every trinket . . . the
India shawl from my back – even down to the very spoons' –
'you break my heart with your books and that boy of yours,
whom you are ruining'. Amelia, like many people, gives presents
in order to buy love, and at times selfishly, but Thackeray makes
the point that she is a discriminating present-giver, unlike
Georgy's grandfather, who is so feverishly anxious to buy the
boy that he gives him adult, inappropriate and corrupting
presents. Jane Osborne's gold watch and chain is a more
affectionate, sad present, and acts also to show a sense of
independence, like Fanny Price's silver knife in *Mansfield Park*.
When she thinks her father disapproves of her giving the watch
to George, she says that it was bought with her 'own money'. To
give presents supposes some possessions – that is partly why
Jemima's present is so moving, because it is not her own.

Amelia's piano, a conspicuous and eloquent object, is made
the title of two chapters : 'How Captain Dobbin Bought a
Piano' and 'Who Played on the Piano Captain Dobbin Bought'.
Dobbin gives it anonymously, to please, and so that it shall not
pass into anyone else's defiling possession. It is an ironic present,
an illusion enjoyed by Amelia, for she thinks George bought it
for her, and is hurt and resentful when the donor turns out to
be Dobbin. Dobbin wanted something back, after all, and minds
very much when Amelia shows her disappointment. The piano
brings out her ingratitude, as a displaced sacred object. It is
saturated with a great deal of feeling by the time it makes its

last appearance: nostalgia, love, thoughtfulness, lack of love, resentment, jealousy, reverence, misplaced gratitude and ingratitude. Objects are focuses and repositories as they pass to and from people in a ritual and personal act, in fiction as in life. But giving in *Vanity Fair* is corrupted, like sex and art, and even the most noble characters are not exempt from the corruption.

Not giving and wrong giving are important, too. George does not give Amelia a bouquet, or the piano. Jos gives money, food and presents lavishly because they are easier to offer than love, sympathy and support. In Brussels he bestows his military-looking clothing on his servant Isidore in panic and desperation. There seems to be no character in the novel who does not express himself fully in giving, taking, or not giving. *Vanity Fair*, the novel where we should expect gimcracks and fairings, is especially concerned with donation, but there are plenty of examples in the other novels too. Esmond's presentation of the family diamonds to Beatrix is a striking act of possessive, proud and seignioral giving, as the Duke of Hamilton and Beatrix herself both recognize. When she gives them back, in the quarrel about the Pretender, there is the marvellous little detail of a forgotten object, the miniature of the Duke of Hamilton that is accidentally handed over with them. Her mother is alert to this significant accident, and draws attention to it jealously, hurtingly and intelligently. Pen and Ethel signal love, reminiscence, jealousy, anger and hurt, when Ethel says grandly that she may accept a mount from the Marquis of Farintosh and Pen asks if she still rides the pony, Bhurtpore, that his father gave her. Harry Warrington is hurt when he wants to give Theo and Hetty a ball, and Hetty is ungrateful because she is afraid of being too grateful. Colonel Newcome showers presents on Clive, including too much money and a bride. Laura lends Pen the money which she says lovingly she 'owes' Helen, and is very hurt when it is paid back. All these objects, inert but potent, express, relate, connect, separate, wound, signal, speak, implore, banish, demand, embrace, remember, forget, hate and love.

Conspicuous Consumption

Apart from expressing people, the objects in Thackeray are also expressive of a society, its houses, furniture, food, drink, art, culture, taste. Perhaps the best taste in Vanity Fair is Lord Steyne's, as Tom Eaves tells the author :

> 'The Prince and Perdita have been in and out of that door, sir,' he has often told me; 'Marianne Clarke has entered it with the Duke of ———. It conducts to the famous *petits appartements* of Lord Steyne – one, sir, fitted up all in ivory and white satin, another in ebony and black velvet; there is a little banqueting-room taken from Sallust's house at Pompeii, and painted by Cosway – a little private kitchen, in which every saucepan was silver, and all the spits were gold.' (Chap. 47)

Then there is 'the paradise of . . . Court', to which Becky drives with footmen carrying enormous bouquets, magnificent purloined brocade and lace, and clandestine diamonds from two sources, neither admitted by Becky who pleads honest poverty and the hiring of the stones at Mr Polonius's :

> Thus Rawdon knew nothing about the brilliant diamond ear-rings, or the superb brilliant ornament which decorated the fair bosom of his lady; but Lord Steyne, who was in his place at court, as Lord of the Powder Closet, and one of the great dignitaries and illustrious defences of the throne of England, and came up with all his stars, garters, collars, and cordons, and paid particular attention to the little woman, knew whence the jewels came, and who paid for them. (Chap. 48)

Objects, titles, splendour – the emphasis is placed on an excess of property, a perversion of use, an excess of art, as with the silver saucepans, perhaps the most satisfactory item of clandestine but conspicuous consumption in Thackeray. Thackeray can never resist putting the value of possessions, whether costume or works of art, in the perspective of history, and some of the most solid-seeming grandeur in Vanity Fair is discredited at the same time as it is inventoried :

> Bareacres Castle was theirs, too, with all its costly pictures, furniture, and articles of virtu – the magnificent Vandykes; the noble Reynolds pictures; the Lawrence portraits, tawdry and beautiful, and, thirty years ago, deemed as precious as works of real genius; the matchless Dancing Nymph of Canova, for which Lady Bareacre had sate in her youth. . . . (Chap. 49)

There is a journalist in *Vanity Fair*, Mr John Paul Jefferson Jones, who knows 'the service of the table; the size and costume of the servants; . . . the dishes and wines served; the ornaments of the side-board, and the probable value of the plate'. The inventorying and pricing eye is Thackeray's too, and though much has been said about the historical flashbacks of Thackeray, Dickens and George Eliot, Thackeray was probably the only one aware of the datable value of works of art. As someone who thought little of Lawrence, for instance, he would be keen to report, with accuracy, that he had sold in his day but had not lasted. There are several similar allusions to evanescent conspicuous consumption in the novels. Thackeray reports appearances, as one might expect of a painter, illustrator and journalist.

'I have no head above my eye' will not, however, quite do to describe Thackeray's solidity of specification, thought poorly of by Henry James Senior, who took the 'I describe what I see' at its face-value. It is not too much of an exaggeration to say that not only Madame Merle's doctrine of containing and expressing objects, but the basis and design of *The Spoils of Poynton,* was taken for granted by Thackeray, yet in his customarily muted fashion. Every character is given an environment of objects, and they are labelled and priced at current market-value. Many are named commodities, like Lawrence, Canova, certain brands of bad claret. Thackeray knows what clothes, wigs, make-up and foundation garments the characters wear, what the clothes are made of, the type of jewels they wear and where they came from, whether their clothes are clean, dirty, bought, given, borrowed, stolen, made at home, whether they suited them or not. He knows what their cultural appurtenances are too, whether they read Lamartine, like Blanche Amory, or Pope, like Steyne, or the *Arabian Nights*, or Horace, or Smollett's history, or his fiction. Such solid and accurate social detail is one of the things that makes all his novels historical. It also makes him, as a chronicler of surfaces, as informative and as rich as Ben Jonson or Zola.

When Virginia Woolf accuses Arnold Bennett of giving us mere facts about costumes and objects, in her famous essay *Mr Bennett and Mrs Brown*, she fails to see the psychological and social eloquence of Bennett's surfaces. At his best, in *The Old Wives' Tale* or *Anna of the Five Towns*, Bennett is a lesser Thackeray, and what Virginia Woolf said about him was as useful and as inaccurate as what Henry James Senior said about Thackeray.[5] Thackeray's objects are presented imaginatively, being related to each other, and to his persons and events, like love, the smell of cooking, Spinoza, and the typewriter in Eliot's famous illustration of imaginative unity. The documented environment tells us, first, about the individuals who live in it. Lord Steyne's silver saucepan tells us a great deal about his sensuality, though his description of his anchorite's bed needs to be put beside it, probably as an image of exhaustion and ennui. Thackeray tells us what people's tastes are, when they started to collect and buy, what for, whether for show, pleasure, waste, investment, creation, seduction. Above all, because this is sociology in the form of fiction, the environment and envelope of objects are pyschologically expressive and morally emblematic. The consumption is not only economically but psychologically conspicuous.

James's mistake about Thackeray is perhaps explained, as at least an understandable one, if we reflect that one can say a great deal about Thackeray's presentation of environment and objects without using the word symbol. There are plenty of symbols in the novel – the painting of the Prodigal Son, the *Don Giovanni* statue music, the part of Clytemnestra – but these are less important than the primary solid state of things. The symbols, useful in a way as decorations, intensifiers, metaphors, are nonetheless dispensable. Marvellous and accurate, of course, to see Lord Steyne as Don Giovanni, but not so necessary as to perceive that in the last scene in the opera Mozart, like Thackeray, is invoking common experience of life and death, the flesh and hell, hospitality and unwanted guest. The last supper of the Don is expressive of his moral and psychological state – sensual, reckless, flaunting, afraid, blasphemous – like the backgrounds or environments of the characters in Thackeray. Thackeray describes what he sees, providing what he praised in the eighteenth-century novelists, a portrait of society. He creates the exterior of the past, the costumes, wigs, paint, furniture, food,

[5] Henry James Senior met Thackeray in America in 1852, and in August 1853 he confided to Ralph Waldo Emerson that 'Thackeray could not see beyond his eyes, and has no ideas, and merely is a sounding-board against which his experiences thump and resound: he is the merest boy'. (Ralph Waldo Emerson, *Journals*, Vol. VIII, p. 393) I am indebted to Gordon Ray (*Letters*, Vol. III, p. 142) for this reference.

roads, towns, transport – all that has dated. Thackeray, with
the historian's concern for documentation and the painter's eye
for the visible world, consciously preserves these datable details
in his novels which are, nonetheless, fictions. As such, they work
through people and humours as well as manners, morals as well
as costumes. Thackeray knows that the man's envelope is part
of him, defines the degree of his freedom, the extent of his
conditioning, his taste and loves, his susceptibility to the outsides
of others, or to the objects of trade, religion and beauty. His is
not only a history, but a sociology and a moral psychology, of the
world of objects. That world presents conspicuous consumption
as lucidly and damningly as Veblen. It shows a Babylon or a
Vanity Fair as sententiously and didactically as the Book of
Daniel or Bunyan, but it brings allegory into the social picture of
an actual age, indeed of several ages, though the money and
trade ethic determines them all. As a novelist, Thackeray is
concerned with particulars, and though objects alone cannot
particularize – as Virginia Woolf realized so introvertedly and
fervently that she could scarcely read the novels of Bennett –
they are part of the individual.

Becky's dry handkerchief which she waves to the departing
Rawdon; J.J.'s palette, 'the great shield painted of many colours'
and lit by the 'bright northern light' of his studio; the 'great,
large, square, gilt Peerage,[6] open at FARINTOSH, MARQUIS
OF——'; 'the great callous mirror' that, reflecting Rosey no
more, mirrors only her victorious mother; and those other
looking-glasses reflecting loneliness, one so terrifying Madame
de Florac, *née* Higgs, that she covers it over but still fancies
her image behind, turning as she turns in her bed; the repeated
reflections of the dead and stately Osborne dining-room, the
greenish tinge the Marquis of Farintosh saw in his reflection in
the Brighton mirror, while Clive draws jealous caricatures of
fictitious ancestors; the coco-nut tree; the star that Pitt Crawley
does not wear and the scar Lord Steyne does; little Rose
Crawley's lovely lilac dress torn by the Wiltshire sow; Betty
Martin's yellow shawl, green boots, and light blue hat with red
feather; Mrs Crawley's fat lolling spaniel; Ethel's dress of amber
and blue shot silk, remembered by Clive; Miss Swartz's amber-

---

[6] Thackeray's use of titles as illustrated here, and his use of address in
Chap. 1, show his analysis of another 'power' and 'vanity'.

coloured satin, turquoise bracelets and 'all sorts of tags and gimcracks' : all these objects do more than define money, class and
occupation, they also show emotion, are saturated with feeling
and value. Sometimes it is the absence of feeling that shows, as in
that dry handkerchief and the clipped roses. More often it is a
positive charge : the frightening mirrors, as lonely in Thackeray
as in Auden, the over-loved clothes, the old dress Clive remembers
and the great flounces on the new one that Ethel smooths as
love admits defeat by the 'great world'. There are a few professional objects, tools of the trade, mostly possessed by writers
and painters. Thackeray was accused of having too little respect
for his profession in *Pendennis*, but while he shows all professions
debased or distorted by trade, he does at times suggest a kind
of pastoral sense of honour in the practice of the arts, more, it
must be admitted, in painting than writing. In this respect he
is like George Eliot, particularly in her last novels, but she
repeats and reveres all the arts as well as the sciences and trades.

There are some vivid objects in Thackeray's lectures on *The
English Humourists*, solid details which he was remembering,
not inventing : a young lady taking a pinch of snuff and putting
her knife in her mouth, goose after almond pudding, Pope
stitched every morning into his buckram, the Duchess of Marlborough's ivory figure of the dead Congreve, made to bow and
nod in agreement when she spoke. Such details of manners and
humours are startlingly solid and mobile. They draw attention,
also, to Thackeray's occasional use of objects in similes which
describe his author's qualities. The solid envelope presented in
The English Humourists is made up not only of historical things,
but of imagined ones, like the Dresden china and the Italian
hurdy-gurdy used in Thackeray's definition of the humour and
spirit of Gay. It must be said, too, that the effect is often
cumulative, like the detailed descriptions of all the food, in order
of consumption, or the striking comment that all the wits were
fat, except for Pope : 'Swift was fat; Addison was fat; Steele
was fat; Gay and Thomson were preposterously fat – all that
fuddling and punch-drinking, that club and coffee-house boozing,
shortened the lives and enlarged the waistcoats of the men of that
age.' This draws one's attention to Thackeray's interest in fat
people in the novels, especially in *Vanity Fair*, where there is
the sad, lonely, vain, tight-laced and brilliantly attired fat of

Jos Sedley, and all the fat pets, fat footmen and fat coachmen.[7]

As well as dispersing details to create a cumulative effect, Thackeray sometimes concentrates them in a single incident or scene. Out of many set-pieces, which tell us something of the time, the class and the nature of the human beings in the foreground, I choose two. In a letter from America,[8] Thackeray observes that the *nouveaux riches* take some time to learn good taste, and his illustration of rich bad taste is as memorable, I think, as James's descriptions of Mrs Lowder's furniture and household goods in *The Wings of the Dove*. Like them, it glitters, is heavily ornamented, declares its wealth, is ostentatious. Unlike them, belonging to an earlier period (the 1840s), it is bad taste in a lighter, French style. This is the wealth of the Newcomes, extravagantly transmuted and displayed flamboyantly in objects:

The fine house in Tyburnia was completed by this time, as gorgeous as money could make it. How different it was from the old Fitzroy Square Mansion with its ramshackle furniture, and spoils of brokers' shops, and Tottenham Court Road odds and ends! An Oxford Street upholsterer had been let loose in the yet virgin chambers; and that inventive genius had decorated them with all the wonders his fancy could devise. Roses and Cupids quivered on the ceilings, up to which golden arabesques crawled from the walls; your face (handsome or otherwise) was reflected by countless looking-glasses, so multiplied and arranged as, as it were, to carry you into the next street. You trod on velvet, pausing with respect in the centre of the carpet, where Rosey's cipher was worked in the sweet flowers which bear her name. What delightful crooked legs the chairs had! What corner-cupboards there were filled with Dresden gimcracks, which it was part of this little woman's business in life to purchase! What étagères, and bonbonières, and chiffonnières! What awfully bad pastels there were on the walls! What frightful Boucher and Lancret shepherds and shepherdesses leered over the portières! What velvet-bound volumes, mother-of-pearl albums, inkstands representing beasts of the field, priedieu chairs, and wonderful nick-nacks I can recollect! There was the most magnificent piano, though Rosey seldom sang any of her six songs now; and when she kept her couch at a certain most

---

[7] I am grateful to Carole Fabian for drawing my attention to the almost unobtrusive fat in the first sentence of the novel.

[8] *Letters*, Vol. III, p. 143.

interesting period, the good Colonel, ever anxious to procure amusement for his darling, asked whether she would not like a barrel-organ grinding fifty or sixty favourite pieces, which a bearer could turn? (Chap. 63)

Some of Thackeray's favourite objects are here, mirrors, flowers and pastoral figures, and they are all directed towards the ironic presentation of a love-nest for Clive created out of money, bad taste and love. Clive is a painter in a pretentious and ridiculous environment, hence the insistence on the intricate horrors. He is a fish out of water in marriage, Rosey's shallow sweetness making the roses especially thorny. But the description is also an indictment of contemporary expensive tastelessness, and as usual Thackeray knows where all the furniture was bought, who designed and executed the decorations.

My other *morceau de musée* comes from *Esmond*, and is displayed by Beatrix. It is even more transitory than Rosey's fine house, and it is worth noticing that Thackeray, like the Book of Daniel, likes to show the vanity and transience of big and heavy objects, gold and silver plate as well as gimcracks. We should notice too, the emphasis on ludicrously bad art, and the emphasis on personal and class-emblems. Rosey's cipher is stamped on the velvet carpet, though her image has not taken more deeply or personally. Similarly, Beatrix's coronet is one she never actually gets, like the other gradual ascending signs, the gilt crown of a duchess and, of course, the crown.[9] This miscellany of objects surrounds her during her betrothal to the Duke of Hamilton, and here Esmond has come to tell her that he has been killed in a duel :

> . . . If a satire upon human vanity could be needed, that poor soul afforded it in the altered company and occupations in which Esmond found her. For days before, her chariot had been rolling the street from mercer to toyshop – from goldsmith to laceman : her taste was perfect, or at least the fond bridegroom had thought so, and had given entire authority over all tradesmen, and for all the plate, furniture, and equipages, with which his Grace the

[9] The baron's coronet and the duchess's crown had appeared in succession on the shagreen case for the diamonds Esmond gave her (Bk 3, Chap. 10). But in Bk 3, Chap. 7, Thackeray omits the latter insignia in his description, the box being stamped simply with a coronet.

Ambassador wished to adorn his splendid mission. She must have her picture by Kneller, a duchess not being complete without a portrait, and a noble one he made, and actually sketched in, on a cushion, a coronet which she was about to wear. She vowed she would wear it at King James the Third's coronation, and never a princess in the land would have become ermine better. Esmond found the ante-chamber crowded with milliners and toyshop women, obsequious goldsmiths with jewels, salvers, and tankards; and mercers' men with hangings, and velvets, and brocades. My Lady Duchess Elect was giving audience to one famous silversmith from Exeter Change, who brought with him a great chased salver, of which he was pointing out the beauties as Colonel Esmond entered. 'Come,' says she, 'Cousin, and admire the taste of this pretty thing.' I think Mars and Venus were lying in the golden bower, that one gilt Cupid carried off the war-god's casque – another his sword – another his great buckler, upon which my Lord Duke of Hamilton's arms with ours were to be engraved – and a fourth was kneeling down to the reclining goddess with the ducal coronet in his hands. . . . (Bk 3, Chap. 6)

The running title is 'Omnia Vanitas'.[10] The merchants, milliners and silversmith bridge the world of objects and characters, themselves reduced most plainly to mere purveyors of objects. The scene is a great visual set-piece. It is also a melodramatic illustration of the running title, with Beatrix pointing out the 'fine carving of the languid prostrate Mars' and 'the arch graces

[10] Unfortunately, the Penguin edition of *Esmond* does not include Thackeray's running titles which are sensitive pointers to theme, structure and mood.

of the Cupids' : Thackeray does not make the point through the objects alone, and in a highly explicit fashion suggests the irony of 'the warrior dead in his chamber, his servants and children weeping', that reversal of the amorous design. Beatrix lifts up the salver, its brilliance and hers lit – and conflated – by the 'flambeaux', and Esmond makes his interpretation, calling her Herodias. She drops the plate, but the 'eager goldsmith' picks it up, and we have already been told about the transitoriness of possession and the adaptability of trade and unfinished chasing : 'The next time Mr Esmond saw that piece of plate, the arms were changed, the ducal coronet had been replaced by a viscount's; it formed part of the fortune of the thrifty goldsmith's own daughter, when she married my Lord Viscount Squanderfield two years later'. The emphasis here is on rank's purchase of power, in direct contrast to the aesthetic emphasis in *The Newcomes*, but Thackeray is also interested here in bad taste, flaunting and highly ornate. As an account of trade and consumption, this is highly compressed, eloquent satire. As an episode and a crisis in the plot, it involves the objects dramatically,[11] both as symbols and false idols, summing up Beatrix's idolatry, mercenariness and frivolity. The attachment to toys – though a historic detail – allows Thackeray to comment on immaturity and the struggle against ennui, which we find still present in Beatrix on her terrible reappearance, as an old woman, in *The Virginians*.

Thackeray's world of expressive objects is part of his satire and moral preaching, but a visually and dramatically expressive part, making it superfluous for him to analyse and comment. He does not say, in either of the last two instances, that here we have conspicuous consumption, people reduced to objects by the desire, selling and buying of objects, people pathetically and frustratedly showering objects on each other in generosity and love, people preying on each other for objects, and so on. A certain irony is made articulate by the narrator – Rosey's cipher, the Duke's arms, and the Mars and Cupid – but the larger irony is left to speak for itself, both in such clusters of appurtenances and in the presentation of objects throughout the novels.

---

[11] Two particularly interesting modern chroniclers of the object-world are Hermann Hesse in *Steppenwolf* and Scott Fitzgerald in *The Great Gatsby*.

Moreover, the objects colour and people the world, make it scenic and concrete, both as a piece of critical social analysis, and as a drama. Thackeray has been accused of presenting people remotely, or of an over-panoramic treatment. One of the many answers to such objections may be made by drawing attention to this concreteness. It does not reside in catalogues, or always in very great visual detail, but in bringing people into relation with the world of objects, or showing that their relations to each other, and sometimes even their solitary passions, are inseparable from the environment of objects. That this environment is so reductive, even so hostile, is another mark of the social diagnosis through accurate portraiture. And although it varies, historically, from the time of Queen Anne to the early nineteenth century, it is still a familiar object-world, even now.

I began with some objects from Thackeray's personal experience, and I shall return to them, briefly, in a last word about his most profound presentation of surfaces, an essential implicit aspect of his social satire and his drama of social conditioning. Thackeray was a *viveur*, he was a visual artist, a painter, with a strong aesthetic sense. His appetites, his creativity and his taste led him to savour and appreciate objects, food, drink, clothes, pictures, ornaments, furniture, houses. But there is no good appreciation of objects in the novels. He was also an affectionate, even sentimental man, but nowhere in his writing does he show a disinterested affection for an object – like Silas Marner's feeling for his brown jug. He was a professional writer, a craftsman, but there is only one example that I recall in the novels of the feeling for the tools of the trade. In the personal life, objects might be savoured, loved, respected. In his fiction, in the exploration of society by the explorations of chronicle and description, the objects emerge tainted. Relics, icons, presents, costly articles, they show the greed and heartlessness of a period of aggression and rapid expansion.

CHAPTER FIVE

The Comic Feast

Conspicuous consumption of valuable goods is a means of reputability to the gentleman of leisure. As wealth accumulates on his hands, his own unaided effort will not avail to sufficiently put his opulence in evidence by this method. The aid of friends and competitors is therefore brought in by resorting to the giving of valuable presents and expensive feasts and entertainments. Presents and feasts had probably another origin than that of naïve ostentation, but they acquired their utility for this purpose very early, and they have retained that character to the present; so that their utility in this respect has now long been the substantial ground on which these usages rest. Costly entertainments, such as the potlatch or the ball, are peculiarly adapted to serve this end. The competitor with whom the entertainer wishes to institute a comparison is, by this method, made to serve as a means to the end. He consumes vicariously for his host at the same time that he is a witness to the consumption of that excess of good things which his host is unable to dispose of single-handed, and he is also made to witness his host's facility in etiquette.

Thorstein Veblen, *The Theory of the Leisure Class*, Chap. 4

'I smile,' says the author in *The Newcomes*, 'as I think how much dining has been already commemorated in these veracious pages; but the story is an everyday record; and does not dining form a certain part of the pleasure and business of every day?' Once more, there is a certain distinction between Thackeray's personal and his fictional presentation, between the record of feasts in his letters and in the novels, where he is standing back from the personal experience, animating the portrait of manners, objectifying and moralizing the pleasure. There is not quite the contrast there was between the objects in life and in the novels, for the biographical record is not unequivocally epicurean. Thackeray enjoyed the 'great world', as he constantly calls it in *The Newcomes*, but his record of wining and dining shows the usual number of headaches, upsets, ennuis and quarrels, as well as appreciation of the pleasures of society. In one letter to his American friends, the Baxters, written in June 1853, when he was writing *The Newcomes*, he makes this revealing comment:

> I am tired of the great world pretty well, and am as glad to get quit of it after 3 weeks idleness and lounging and gourmandizing as if I had been born a Marquis. I think of the future for my girls and what they are to do in the tramp and bustle of that London life, and have a mind to cut the *belle société* altogether, and go and live among my equals. Well they have their tramp & bustle too, their crowding to parties long dinners squeezy balls, flatterers toadies and what not just as in the Grandee world.
>
> (*Letters*, Vol. III, p. 279)

Thackeray's portrait hangs over the mantelpiece in the Reform Club, where he used to stand, and an aura of well-dined and wined mid-Victorian conviviality hangs over his image as a novelist. If we remember Dickens as the great dramatizer of family festivity, Christmas, Dingley Dell and the Fezziwigs' Ball, we remember Thackeray as the author of the famous apostrophe to claret in *The Adventures of Philip* and the recorder of great banquets, balls and feasts. Gordon Ray begins his chapter called 'The Great World'[1] by saying that 'it was Thackeray's good fortune to come to know London society during the final period of aristocratic predominance in English life' and he gives us a chronicle of the range of entertainments, their sexual and class and professional typology, and comments: ' . . . it may be fairly said that London society embodied for the rest of the nation all that splendour, luxury, and personal privilege could do towards making life agreeable and exciting'. But his most appreciative comments on such fascinations of the great world come perhaps

[1] *Life*, Vol. 2, Chap. 2.

from Henry James, 'if it kept the gods themselves for the time in good humour, one was willing enough, or at least I was, to be on the side of the gods', and from Santayana: 'English high life . . . at once established itself in my regard side by side with ancient and Catholic life as one of the high lights of history.' Although Ray chronicles Thackeray's good company, and his appreciation of it, the chronicle has here and there some critical tones, 'a parcel of good-natured tom-fools', but his main point is that Thackeray came to feel at home in it, unlike Dickens, Tennyson and Charlotte Brontë. It is not my purpose to attempt to refute this view, which is supported by Locker-Lampson's testimonial to Thackeray's 'sensibility': ' . . . he delighted in luxuriously furnished and well-lighted rooms, good music, excellent wines and cookery, exhilarating talk, gay and airy gossip, pretty women and their toilettes, and refined and noble manners, le bon gout, le ris, l'aimable liberté. The amenities of life and the traditions stimulated his imagination', and Thackeray's own joking words to Lady Blessington, 'I reel from dinner party to dinner party – I wallow in turtle and swim in Shampang', are also backed, rather more pointedly, by a *Punch* issue of 1850, where he says that 'it is natural that a man should like the society of people well-to-do in the world; who make their houses pleasant, who gather pleasant persons about them, who have fine pictures on their walls, pleasant books in their libraries, pleasant parks and town and country houses, good cooks and good cellars: if I were coming to dine with you, I would rather have a good dinner than a bad one'.

Gordon Ray is perfectly right to insist on Thackeray as *bon viveur*, and right too, perhaps, to suggest that his attitude to London society remained critical but 'his estimate of it changed drastically as he came to know it better'; but it is my contention that Thackeray the novelist changed very much less drastically, if at all, and that his novels, from *Vanity Fair* to *The Adventures of Philip*, are very much more concerned with the critique of worldliness than his biographer suggests. But even in the dazzling and perhaps fascinating social record, there are skeletons and writings on the wall: gossip, uncultivated and ignorant remarks about Thackeray himself, and Thackeray's touchiness. His social record shows a number of insults, quarrels and darknesses, like the occasion, which is a fairly common instance of life imitating fiction, when Thackeray (like his own Dobbin, only a little later) visited a sale, at Gore House, and gave the valet, 'not a powdered one but a butler a whatdyoucall it' a pound, 'Ah it was a strange sad picture of Wanaty Fair'. Thackeray's participation would seem to have been as partial and critical as that of Dobbin, inclined to spill wine, Esmond, touchy and melancholy, or George Warrington, the three characters who illustrate Thackeray's tempered and classless 'gentleman' but who are markedly ill at ease in 'good company'.

Thackeray writes against the great world as one who knows its excesses and ennuis from the inside, but also, from time to time, as one who likes to distinguish *la belle société* from the smaller world, where the company is not so good and the claret, food and service decidedly inferior. Just as he occasionally likes to attack the vain things and tastes of the great world by criticizing a Newcome drawing-room or a Queen Anne salver, so at times he attacks not the feast but the inferior feast. He is criticizing indulgence, but also criticizing shams, imitations and pretentiousness, though at times, perhaps, the emphatic revulsion of taste rather distracts our attention from the general criticism of vanity and indulgence.

Thackeray's usual attitude to feasts is critical; he never wholeheartedly celebrates fictional good wine, food and company, as at times he does in his letters. Lord Steyne's silver saucepans were suspect, and so is the *gourmandise* of Dr Firmin, the splendid villainous doctor and lady-killer in *Philip*. This description of his meal is sinister in its richness, and the twinkling diamond, pretty hand, creaming wine and ice-pail combine to suggest something corrupt :

We could see Firmin smiling on his neighbour with his blandest melancholy, and the waiters presently bearing up the dishes which the doctor had ordered for his own refection. *He* was no lover of mutton chops and coarse sherry, as I knew, who had partaken of many a feast at his board. I could see the diamond twinkle on his pretty hand, as it daintily poured out creaming wine from the ice-pail by his side – the liberal hand that had given me many a sovereign when I was a boy.

'I can't help liking him,' I said to my companion, whose scornful eyes were now and again directed towards his colleague. 'This port is very sweet. Almost all port is sweet now.' (Chap. 3)

The reply is marvellously directed to Firmin as well as the port.
The dining-room and drawing-room express the same sinister
and grotesque handsomeness :

> Everything in Dr Firmin's house was as handsome as might be,
> and yet somehow the place was not cheerful. One's steps fell
> noiselessly on the faded Turkey carpet; the room was large, and
> all save the dining-table in a dingy twilight. The picture of Mrs
> Firmin looked at us from the wall, and followed us about with
> wild violet eyes. Philip Firmin had the same violet odd bright
> eyes, and the same coloured hair of an auburn tinge; in the
> picture it fell in long wild masses over the lady's back as she
> leaned with bare arms on a harp. Over the sideboard was the
> doctor, in a black velvet coat and a fur collar, his hand on a
> skull, like Hamlet. Skulls of oxen, horned, with wreaths, formed
> the cheerful ornaments of the cornice. On the side-table glittered
> a pair of cups, given by grateful patients, looking like receptacles
> rather for funereal ashes than for festive flowers or wine. Brice,
> the butler, wore the gravity and costume of an undertaker. The
> footman stealthily moved hither and thither, bearing the dinner
> to us; we always spoke under our breath whilst we were eating it.
> 'The room don't look more cheerful of a morning when the
> patients are sitting here, I can tell you,' Phil would say; indeed,
> we could well fancy that it was dismal. The drawing-room had
> a rhubarb-coloured flock paper (on account of the governor's
> attachment to the shop, Master Phil said), a great piano, a harp
> smothered in a leather-bag in the corner, which the languid
> owner now never touched; and everybody's face seemed scared
> and pale in the great looking-glasses, which reflected you over and
> over again into the distance, so that you seemed to twinkle off
> right through the Albany into Piccadilly. (Chap. 2)

On other occasions in *Philip*, Pendennis's attack on hypocrisy
and vanity is a direct onslaught, as in Chapter 4, 'A Genteel
Family', where gentility is completely defined and satirized in a
closely documented account of a dinner-party. The chapter opens
with a general question about the morality and economics of
keeping up appearances, of 'seeming and being in the world'.
He observes, 'Sometimes it is hard to say where honest pride
ends and hypocrisy begins. To obtrude your poverty is mean
and slavish . . .' and moves into a comparison of 'noble pride'

and 'shabby swindling', in the cases of two nonce characters, Eugenia and Jezebella. Jezebella leads straight into the Twysdens' dining-room :

> When I sit at poor Jezebella's table, and am treated to her sham bounties and shabby splendour, I only feel anger for the hospitality, and that dinner, and guest, and host, are humbugs together.
> Talbot Twysden's dinner-table is large, and the guests most respectable. There is always a bigwig or two present, and a dining dowager who frequents the greatest houses. There is a butler who offers you wine; there's a *menu du diner* before Mrs Twysden; and to read it you would fancy you were at a good dinner. It tastes of chopped straw. Oh, the dreary sparkle of that feeble champagne; the audacity of that public-house sherry; the swindle of that acrid claret; the fiery twang of that clammy port! I have tried them all, I tell you! It is sham wine, a sham dinner, a sham welcome, a sham cheerfulness, among the guests assembled. I feel that that woman eyes and counts the cutlets as they are carried off the tables; perhaps watches that one which you try to swallow. She has counted and grudged each candle by which the cook prepares the meal. Does her big coachman fatten himself on purloined oats and beans, and Thorley's food for cattle? Of the rinsings of those wretched bottles the butler will have to give a reckoning in the morning. Unless you are of the very great *monde*, Twysden and his wife think themselves better than you are, and seriously patronize you. They consider it is a privilege to be invited to those horrible meals to which they gravely ask the greatest folks in the country. I actually met Winton there – the famous Winton – the best dinner-giver in the world (ah, what a position for a man!). I watched him, and marked the sort of wonder which came over him as he tasted and sent away dish after dish, glass after glass. 'Try that Château Margaux, Winton!' calls out the host. 'It is some that Bottleby and I imported.' Imported! I see Winton's face as he tastes the wine, and puts it down. He does not like to talk about that dinner. He has lost a day. Twysden will continue to ask him every year; will continue to expect to be asked in return, with Mrs Twysden and one of his daughters; and will express his surprise loudly at the club, saying, 'Hang Winton! Deuce take the fellow! He has sent me no game this year!' When foreign dukes and princes arrive, Twysden straightway collars them, and invites them to his house. (Chap. 4)

Two quotations may stand for Thackeray's attitude, one from
'Before the Curtain', in *Vanity Fair*, where he promises 'a great
quantity of eating and drinking, making love and jilting, laugh-

ing and the contrary, smoking, cheating, fighting, dancing, and
fiddling'; and another from his most severe image of depravity,
in the splendid lecture on Congreve and Addison :

There is life and death going on in everything : truth and lies
always at battle. Pleasure is always warring against self-restraint.
Doubt is always crying Psha, and sneering. . . . I have read two
or three of Congreve's plays over before speaking of him; and
my feelings were rather like those, which I daresay most of us
have had, at Pompeii, looking at Sallust's house and the relics
of an orgy, a dried wine-jar or two, a charred supper-table, the
breast of a dancing-girl pressed against the ashes, the laughing
skull of a jester, a perfect stillness round about, as the cicerone
twangs his moral, and the blue sky shines calmly over the ruin.

(*The English Humourists*, Lecture 2)

For Victorian visitors to Italy, Pompeii provided a new image of the *memento mori*, or skeleton at the feast, perhaps as memorably put in Thackeray's account of his response to Congreve as in Trimalchio's silver articulated skeleton. Petronius, though, was introducing the bone to the flesh in order to encourage good appetite, and this *carpe diem* note is what Thackeray calls 'Pagan' in 'poor Congreve's theatre': 'Enjoy, enjoy, enjoy! Would you know the *segreto per esser felice*? Here it is, in a smiling mistress and a cup of Falernian.' It is Thackeray's comment, outside the pretended pagan quotation from Congreve, from Harlequin and from 'godless old' Punch, that hears the dirge, sees lights burn dim, and 'the cup drops on the floor'. It is Thackeray who admires the wit of Congreve, but observes, 'ah! it's a weary feast, that banquet of wit where no love is.[2] It palls very soon; sad indigestions follow it and lonely blank headaches in the morning'.

He has two phrases for this 'comic dance of the last century': 'the weary feast' and 'the comic feast'. And although there are only two novels concerned with that particular eighteenth-century comic feast, *Esmond*, which does little with it, and *The Virginians*, which does a little more, its pattern, though not its paganism, appears in all Thackeray's novels. His feasts are nearly always comic and weary. Sometimes they are very like Congreve's, showing 'the very worst company in the world', though more often they show something enjoyable, something ceremonial, even something hospitable, but with a flaw in the enjoyment, the ceremony and the hospitality. Thackeray does not show 'Death and Fate . . . at the gate', as he does in his description of the pagan feast, nor does he have Trimalchio's skeleton, but he has an interesting comic equivalent and substitute.

There are, as a matter of fact, some real skeletons in Thackeray, but they usually come in cupboards, not at feasts. They have a similar function, though, to the skeleton at the feast, and in presenting a domestic flaw or discord they provide a good model of the kind of comedy I have in mind. Such scenes which create a contrast between domestic storm and the appearance of peaceful welcome to the guest belong to Thackeray's analysis of the difficulties and hypocrisies of family life and the house-

---

[2] Another reminder of his criticisms of wit in Becky and Steyne.

hold. The spurious harmony of the house of Castlewood can
stand as an example:

> In houses, where, in place of that sacred, inmost flame of love,
> there is discord at the centre, the whole household becomes
> hypocritical, and each lies to his neighbour. The husband (or it
> may be the wife) lies when the visitor comes in, and wears a grin
> of reconciliation before him. The wife lies (indeed, her business
> is to do that, and to smile, however much she is beaten), swallows
> her tears, and lies to her lord and master; lies in bidding little
> Jacky respect dear papa; lies in assuring grandpapa that she is
> perfectly happy. The servants lie, wearing grave faces behind
> their master's chair, and pretending to be unconscious of the
> fighting; and so, from morning till bed-time, life is passed in
> falsehood. (*Esmond*, Bk 1, Chap. 11)

But Thackeray is not primarily concerned to criticize marriage
as an institution. The false fellowship of society at large is his
target.

The false harmony usually makes its appearance in the
descriptions of the feasts, dinners, balls and other festivities that
form a very large part of the social action and scenery of
Thackeray's novels. What goes wrong with the entertainments of
Vanity Fair are matters of common social experiences. Once
more, the satiric theme is implicit and cumulative, though more
conspicuously dramatized than the satire of the objects. The
feast or party naturally lends itself to scenic and dramatic
treatment, though of course it can be and sometimes is narrated
in summary, or presented piecemeal. What goes wrong reveals
the fragility of entertainments: the physical indulgences offered
by food, drink and mixed company, can go too far, fail or leave
a bad taste; the grace of social relationships, good company and
novelty can end in discord instead of harmony; the entertainments of conversation, wit and heightened social awareness can
turn into ennui, or aggression, because of the wrong people or
the wrong mood; the surface ceremony can easily become trivial
and false.

The parties in *Vanity Fair* are all marked by a gross failure
in ceremony. The very first little festive occasion in the novel,
the farewell to Amelia with seed-cake and wine, is briefly described: it is immediately followed by Becky's various floutings

of ceremony. The first proper festive occasion is Becky's first dinner at the Sedleys', which is unceremonious for two reasons, because the company is slightly less than polite (not the great world, this, but tradespeople in Russell Square) and because the dinner is being used for Becky's clandestine purposes. Thackeray admits that this is scarcely uncommon : 'What causes respectable parents to take up their carpets, set their houses topsy-turvy, and spend a fifth of their year's income in ball suppers and iced champagne?' The answer, of course, is the marriage-market, and Rebecca has to manage her affairs for herself. The dinner brings out the worst in Becky but she is given a comic punishment. 'Capital . . . Mother it's as good as my own curries in India,' says Joseph, in the role of glutton, 'his face quite red with the delightful exercise of gobbling'; 'Oh, I must try some, if it is an Indian dish,' she says, in the role of polite but predatory guest; 'Do you find it as good as everything else from India?' asks Mr Sedley as the heartless host, 'a coarse man, from the Stock Exchange, where they love all sorts of practical jokes'. However, Becky swallows her mortification 'as well as she had the abominable curry' and good-temperedly makes a joke about the peppered cream-tarts in the *Arabian Nights* which endears her to her host. The ladies retire, and the lack of ceremony concludes with the stockbroker falling asleep while his son tells an Indian anecdote and consumes a bottle of claret, two plates of strawberries and cream, and twenty-four rout cakes.

Next comes the visit to Vauxhall. The first attempt is frustrated by a thunderstorm, but eventually the real party of pleasure takes place. Dobbin is introduced as clumsy and in hideous uniform, and George and Mrs Sedley recall how he broke a punch-bowl over Mrs Flamingo's crimson silk gown when he was a boy, 'What a gawky it was!' The preliminary dinner-party passes uneventfully, except for talk about 'war and glory' and Jos's compulsive gobbling and drinking. In the next chapter, 'Vauxhall' (Chap. 6), Dobbin is left, odd man out, to look after the shawls and to pay for the whole party, and he tries to hum Amelia's tune and laughs at his own bad singing while George and Amelia go off together. Rebecca and Jos do not enjoy themselves, and Jos's *gourmandise* in drinking the whole bowl of rack punch not only makes sure that the proposal to Becky shall not take place, but almost ends in riot, as he sings

his drunken song and attracts a great deal of rowdy applause :
'Brayvo, Fat un!', 'Angcore, Daniel Lambert!' 'What a figure
for the tight-rope!' The party breaks up in disarray, with Becky
humiliated as Jos embraces her and shouts, 'Stop, my dearest,
diddle-diddle-darling'. Scarcely the great world, but a vivid
image of social mixture, disharmony, discomfort, noise, muddle,
loneliness, gluttony and entertainment turned sour. Jos's hang-
over next day is inevitable, but the point has already been made.
It was a comic feast and a weary one.

It sets the pattern for all the feasts in *Vanity Fair*. In Brussels,
before Waterloo, there is the gaiety of opera, dinner-parties,
drives, gambling, and the great ball. All the festivities invite
greed, performance, deception and furtive love-making, and
invariably show enjoyment grabbed at someone's expense,
usually Amelia's, sometimes George's too, as Becky and Rawdon
combine to flatter and fleece him.

There are the dinners for Miss Crawley, where the best is
brought out and gluttony and false ceremony mark the occasions.
There are the marvellous dismal dinners at the Osbornes', after
George's death, where ceremony brings out the utter joylessness.
The Osborne dinners start before George decides to marry
Amelia, and their pattern is set when she dines with them,
terrified by old Osborne, who nevertheless has a certain rude
hospitality :

'Dinner!' roared Mr Osborne.
'Mr George isn't come in, sir,' interposed the man.
'Damn Mr George, sir. Am I master of the house? DINNER!'
(Chap. 13)

The meal begins with a 'hushed female company' following
'their dark leader'. The funds are falling, the soup is beastly, the
butler is told to turn away the cook, Billingsgate is suitably
cursed for the fish, and there is silence till George arrives. When
the ladies have retired, he is told by his father while they drink
that he'll have 'no lame duck's daughter'. Amelia in the drawing-
room miserably and hopefully practises his favourite waltzes
(newly imported), and when the butler brings her coffee she
started 'as though it were poison'. The wretchedness and discord
is all the more apparent because this was meant to be a pleasant

dinner-party. Subsequent meals in the same dining-room get much worse, as George is first disapproved, then disinherited, and then dies, while Osborne growls and bullies his way through many grim meals, until he is left, with his daughter, and meals and growls continue. The whole of the family drama is conducted in such dining-scenes, with hardly any exceptions. Here it is hospitability and family relations that are so parodied and upset. Osborne goes on pouring out the old port that is to kill him in the end, with hands that tremble more and more; Jane sits, at the head 'of a table loaded with the grandest plate', a 'middle-aged young lady' who takes dinner with her father in a silence 'seldom broken, except when he swore and was savage, if the cooking was not to his liking'. Thackeray uses the Osborne dinners, neverthe-less, to discriminate cleverly a certain quality of genuineness which is lacking in the entertainments given by his married daughter, Mrs Bullock, who asks her father and sister to her third-rate parties. (The novels give an interesting account of the gradations in entertainments, the rates and ranks of dinners, how the left-overs are served next day, who comes to dinner and who comes afterwards. Thackeray also writes to tell a friend that they find it convenient to give 'double-barrelled' dinner-parties.)[3]

'So she invites her father and sister to a second day's dinner (if those sides, or ontrys, as she calls 'em, weren't served yesterday, I'm d—d. . . .)'

Colonel Newcome, too, is hurt when one sister-in-law invites him to come after dinner, and the other doesn't ask him at all. Family entertainment is an important aspect of Thackeray's presentation of social life. It almost always involves a lack of enjoyment. The Osbornes dine twice a month in a deadly routine with old Dr Gulp and his lady, old Mr Frowser, old Colonel Livermore, and others. In his customary informative way, Thackeray lets us know their age, profession and address. The dinners are pompous, followed by 'solemn' whist : 'Many rich people, whom we poor devils are in the habit of envying, lead contentedly an existence like that above described.' Not that the Osbornes are content. He has sacrificed and lost his son (as

[3] They economized on food and hired service.

E

the Iphigenia clock keeps reminding us) and Jane 'scarcely ever met a man under sixty, and almost the only bachelor who appeared in their society was Mr Smirk, the celebrated lady's doctor'. The comic type-names underline the pathetic comedy of unhappy families.

There are Becky's brilliant little parties, each one a trap for somebody, and with the very best bait. There is the domestic performance put on by Becky for Pitt's benefit, for instance, when she makes him the salmi[4] of Lord Steyne's pheasants (so much more successful than Lady Jane's pie, for Becky is competent and working with the best of materials), and serves him the White Hermitage from Steyne's cellars, which she pretends is a *petit vin blanc* and which brings 'fire into the Baronet's pallid cheeks, and a glow into his feeble frame'. Once more, Thackeray knows what food and drink they are consuming, its value, its origin and its effect. And there are all those other little parties, food and wine supplied from the same source, where Becky advises the young men not to gamble with Rawdon, but in vain. There is always something clandestine in Becky's entertainments, including the last dinner-party without servants present, where Rawdon intrudes : 'A little table with a dinner was laid out – and wine and plate. Steyne was hanging over the sofa on which Becky sate. The wretched woman was in a brilliant full toilette. . . .' (Chap. 53)

The dinner, wine and plate complete the image of debauchery, like those silver saucepans in Steyne's little apartment. It was an expensive occasion, in every way. We should add that less ceremonious meal which Becky hides in her bed, on the occasion of Jos's visit, the brandy bottle and the plate of broken meat, pushed under the covers with a rouge-pot. A far cry from wine, plate, little table, sofa and diamonds. It is part of Becky's amiable powers of survival that she is quite at home with cheap and sluttish living :

> . . . students recruiting themselves with butterbrods and meat; idlers, playing cards or dominoes, on the sloppy, beery tables; tumblers refreshing during the cessation of their performances; – in a word, all the *fumum* and *strepitus* of a German inn in fair time. (Chap. 66)

[4] This must be one of the earliest appearances of the twentieth-century game of 'playing house'.

Even the more harmonious meals go wrong in some way. There is the family Christmas dinner, where little Rawdy says he never eats with his parents at home, and the less embarrassing one when Becky's arrival and acceptance by Pitt are marked by 'Ahem! *Rebecca*, may I give you a wing?' We might add the beer-drinking in the housekeeper's room by the undertakers' men, the great assembly at Gaunt House where Becky is snubbed by the ladies and saved by Lady Gaunt, several gluttonous meals enjoyed by Jos, and one well-intentioned one which Amelia cannot eat and which he and Peggy O'Dowd enjoy instead. Something is wrong with all the 'eating and drinking', whatever the quality of the food and drink. A rare exception is the good coffee Mrs O'Dowd makes for her husband on the morning when he rides off to Waterloo.

I used to think that the failures in parties and pleasures were a special expression of the ironic restive theme of *Vanity Fair*, but it is prominent in all the novels. In *Esmond* dinners and festivities are present but less conspicuous than in the other novels, probably because *Esmond* is the only novel which is primarily a psychological novel, rather than a social satire. The more extroverted forms of the other three depend more on the festive scenes. There are some in *Esmond*, however, as we should expect of the period. There is drama of the passions: the feast of 15th November, 1712, when Esmond dines with Webb, and the Duke of Hamilton disappoints the company, first by his absence, then by his death, which casts gloom over the company, making what was 'meant to be a feast . . . in spite of drink, and talk . . . as dismal as a funeral'. In the course of the awkward and sinister secret meals with the Pretender, there is a particularly interesting threat to ceremony:

> The Prince sat down and bade the ladies sit. The gentlemen remained standing: there was, indeed, but one more cover laid at the table :– 'Which of you will take it?' says he.
> 'The head of our house,' says Lady Castlewood, taking her son's hand, and looking towards Colonel Esmond with a bow and a great tremor of the voice; 'the Marquis of Esmond will have the honour of serving the King.'
> 'I shall have the honour of waiting on his Royal Highness,' says Colonel Esmond, filling a cup of wine, and, as the

fashion of that day was, he presented it to the King on his knee.

'I drink to my hostess and her family,' says the Prince, with no very well-pleased air. . . . (Bk 3, Chap. 9)

There is the pre-arranged quarrel between Lord Mohun and Castlewood, and the later quarrel started by Frank Castlewood, who taunts Mohun for setting himself 'above' him, all at table. There is the great banquet where Webb hands the insulting Gazette to Marlborough by the point of his sword. All these are disrupted ceremonies. There are some happier scenes of drinking with the wits, including a discussion of poetry with Addison over a bottle of burgundy, much drinking with Steele, and one great feast at General Webb's where St John brings in Dr Swift, who is extraordinarily and indulgently confounded by Esmond, whom he has 'insulted' and who has sulkily 'put water in his wine'. This section of literary life is slightly artificial, partly because of the conscientious though skilful allusions, partly because of the difficulty of showing the melancholy and strait-laced Esmond as a young man on the town. Thackeray tells us that 'he liked to *desipere in loco*, neither more nor less than most young men of his age', and even allows him a brief infatuation for the Brace-girdle, but the Horatian quotation and the reference to the actress are not quite enough. Thackeray was no doubt embar-rassed, too, by having to dramatize those pagan orgies he found it easier just to describe in his lectures on the humorists. Orgies, or orgiastic occasions, are indeed rarer in Thackeray's eighteenth-century novels than in the other novels of nineteenth-century life. The feasts are given a special emphasis in each novel. In *Vanity Fair*, the feasts have a mark of the covert and the clandestine. In *Pendennis* – which shows the usual social and emotional vanities but is particularly concerned with class – the festivities are marked by social confusion and blunders. Pen begins by falling in love – more or less – with two women below him in the social scale, and both relationships (or episodes) are shown in awkward festive disharmonies. The first is a very subtle one, where the reader observes what Pen cannot see, blinded by love; as Thackeray knows, there is a certain heart-warming generosity in his blindness, silly though it is. Pen dines on Emily Costigan's 'poy' and the meal is described through his infatuated eyes, and has a certain charm. It is comic, but certainly not weary :

> She arranged the glasses, and laid and smoothed the little cloth, all of which duties she performed with a quiet grace and good humour, which enchanted her guest more and more. The 'poy' arrived from the baker's in the hands of one of the little choir-boy's brothers at the proper hour : and at four o'clock, Pen found himself at dinner – actually at dinner with the handsomest woman in all creation – with his first and only love, whom he had adored ever since when? – ever since yesterday, ever since for ever. He ate a crust of her making, he poured her out a glass of beer, he saw her drink a glass of punch – just one wine-glass full – out of the tumbler which she mixed for her papa. She was perfectly good-natured, and offered to mix one for Pendennis too. It was prodigiously strong; Pen had never in his life drunk so much spirits and water. Was it the punch, or the punch-maker who intoxicated him?
>
> Pen tried to engage her[5] in conversation about poetry and about her profession. He asked her what she thought of Ophelia's madness, and whether she was in love with Hamlet or not? 'In love with such a little ojous wretch as that stunted manager of a Bingley?' She bristled with indignation at the thought. Pen explained it was not of her he spoke, but of Ophelia of the play. 'Oh, indeed; if no offence was meant, none was taken. . . .'
>
> (Chap. 5)

Thackeray refuses to create ideal love-feasts, like the Fezziwig Ball in Scrooge's memory, or Pip's hospitality to Magwitch. Nevertheless, there is a certain beauty about this comic ceremony : it has true hospitality, true appreciation of the food and drink by Emily and her father (Bows is to tell us later that all she really cared about was her dinner). It is also distinguished by perfect happiness on Pen's part. We observe him composing his happiness, of course, ignoring Emily's very healthy appetite

---

[5] This text follows the last (1864) edition of *Pendennis* supervised by Thackeray. In the first (1850) edition, the passage included more about the captain, and indeed one-third of the other revisions of this chapter reduce the prominence of the captain similarly. For 'Pen tried to engage her' the first edition read : 'During dinner, when the captain, whom his daughter treated most respectfully, ceased prattling about himself and his adventures, Pen tried to engage the Fotheringay.'

and seeing her less as a hearty trencher-woman than as a loving daughter, 'cooking dishes to make her old father comfortable, and brewing him drink'. He likewise translates her blank reception of his literary conversation into courtesy, 'How rude it was of me to begin to talk about professional matters, and how well she turned the conversation.' Of course he is to outgrow the illusion, to see Emily as coarse and ignorant, but Thackeray does not present the meal with scathing irony; rather he lets us see its genuineness. Pen is to go further and fare worse.

When he outgrows the infatuation, his education in worldliness begins. Before the dinner with the Fotheringay, we have already met his mentor, Major Pendennis, at a more polite meal, breakfasting on toast, his 'hot newspaper' and his correspondence, at a club in Pall Mall, where he sits at the same table every day, takes breakfast at a quarter past ten, and is dressed 'in the best blacked boots in all London, with a checked morning cravat that never was rumpled till dinner time'. One strand in *Pendennis* is represented by the Major's worldliness and formality at breakfast in his club, another by Pen's dinner on 'poy' and punch, and his intoxicating supper with Foker, which precedes and stimulates his infatuation. We see Pen in high life and low, though the high usually tends to be mixed rather than truly of the 'great world'. One of the later important scenes occurs at Vauxhall, a place of low-life where the mixture of the classes is deliberately brought out. Here Pen meets his second love, Fanny Bolton, also his social inferior, but less able to take care of herself than the Fotheringay. Pen is now very much less likely to suppose that love means marriage and to make a fool of himself. The scene is awkward, confused, exciting: it has the same dark walks, the same illuminations, the same festivity, drink and social mixture that we met in the Vauxhall episode in *Vanity Fair*, but otherwise it is markedly different, altogether more sinister and sexually suggestive, as befits a temptation scene. The rough and tumble in *Vanity Fair* was embarrassing, but nothing more, earned by gluttony and mercenariness. The sense of Dobbin's isolation was wry, no more. But in *Pendennis* there is a marked contrast between Fanny's innocence – socially conscious though it is, and flirtatious, it is still innocent – and Pen's uneasy awareness of Vauxhall's pleasures and their votaries. In the following description of the crowd, for instance, Thackeray contrasts rakes and dubious couples with Fanny's innocent satisfaction :

> And she looked at numbers of other ladies in the place, and at scores of other gentlemen under whose protection they were walking here and there; and she thought that her gentleman was handsomer and grander-looking than any other gent there. Of course there were votaries of pleasure of all ranks in the garden – rakish young surgeons, fast young clerks and commercialists, occasional dandies of the Guard regiments, and the rest. Old Lord Colchicum was there in attendance upon Mademoiselle Carocoline, who had been riding in the ring; and who talked her native French very loud, and used idiomatic expressions of exceeding strength as she walked about, leaning on the arm of his lordship. (Chap. 46)

The word to describe this is not in Thackeray's vocabulary : promiscuous. It fits the social and the sexual suggestions. Many details contribute : little Tom Tufthunt is cast as Leporello to Lord Colchicum's Don Juan. The 'elderly viscount' leers at Pen and his eyes pass 'under the bonnet of Pen's companion'. Tom Tufthunt wags his head. We begin to see why Thackeray spoke of the 'black and dreary passage and wickedness which hide the splendours of Vauxhall from uninitiated men'. Finest touch – Pen is pleased to have Fanny seen by Don Juan.

But there are tawdry touches, too, like the glass buttons, and the 'imaginative' waistcoat and loud trousers of Huxter, whom Pen is not pleased to meet, and snubs. Fanny and Pen watch the fireworks, she 'thrilled and trembled . . . her hand was under his arm still'. Flirtation begins, but Pen tells her 'you mustn't call me anything but sir, or Mr Pendennis, if you like, for we live in very different stations, Fanny!' There is a rather arch suggestion of a kiss, and food, drink and dancing follow. Pen's energetic waltz with Fanny is suddenly interrupted by a bump from Mr Huxter 'and his pink satin young friend'. There is abuse, a row, and the festivity is spoilt, 'to the interruption of the ball, the terror of poor little Fanny, and the immense indignation of Pen'. The ball degenerates into a 'degrading broil' and Pen says handsomely, 'It was my fault to have danced in such a place. I beg your pardon, to have asked you to dance there.' Nothing so gentlemanly as a gentleman being courteous to someone who is not a lady. Hence the title 'Monseigneur s'Amuse', though that has other implications too.

There are several interesting things about the scene, apart from its portrayal of class behaviour. It marks a stage in Pen's progress. He has travelled some distance, socially and sexually, since he was invited to dine with Emily by her father, old Costigan, who plays a comic Pandar figure, sometimes consciously, sometimes not. We are never quite sure what Thackeray is doing with the problem of Pen's sexual innocence, since all male and many female readers would have known well enough how to read between the lines, especially of the dissipated Cambridge period. (Thackeray, of course, makes his celebrated complaint that the Victorian novelist could no longer show a man, as Fielding could.)[6] What Pen is on the brink of in the Fanny episode is not the loss of virginity but the seduction of a poor virgin. (Even Fielding seemed to want to exonerate Tom Jones from the charge of seducing Molly Seagrim, though at the time that was what Tom thought he was doing.) Pen is shown as the young man showing off the girl to the old Don Juan; he is clearly familiar with the Vauxhall dissipations,[7] and is moreover very well acquainted by now with the appropriate behaviour for a young man on the town, as he was not at the beginning of the novel before his uncle and the world had taken a hand in his education. Whereas he was much more innocent than Emily Fotheringay (careful and knowing preserver of a marketable virginity), he is now less innocent than Fanny, spontaneous coquette though Thackeray makes her. He is successfully learning to be a worldling.

There are things wrong with the Vauxhall pleasures, and Pen knows what they are, though Fanny does not. But Thackeray does not maintain what I have called the sinister air of the scene, and indeed he moves from the suggestive crowd-scenes of the beginning into the rough-house and farce of the end. It is possible that *Pendennis*, the novel most inspired by *Tom Jones*, was infected by Fielding's generous use of farce. Overthrows and tumbles are suffered not only by Parson Adams and Joseph Andrews, but even by Sophia Western in her falls and accidents;

---

6 Preface to *Pendennis*.
7 He presumably set out to seek them on the evening of his meeting with Fanny.

they are typical of the free-floating farcical events in Fielding, Sterne and Smollett too, laughable events and usually without symbolic meaning, though threatening, exposing and mocking goodness and virtue. *Pendennis* has more farce than Thackeray's other novels, though there is a certain amount in *Catherine* and *Barry Lyndon*. The farce in the Vauxhall scene seems to be clearly directed to exposing Pen's worldliness, as well as signifying the falsity and fragility of the pleasures of Vanity Fair.

There is another ball in an earlier chapter where Thackeray trips up Pen in the dance, when he was dancing with someone of his own class, Blanche Amory. Thackeray may be using the farcical accident as a gentle way of drawing attention to Pen's ill-matched partnerships, though it seems more likely that he is just showing up worldliness by unceremoniously making a fool of Pen at moments when he thinks he is being rather graceful. Chapter 26 is suitably called 'Contains Some Ball-Practising'. Its ball is a very good dramatic scene, containing the promising drama of Pen, for once jealous of Laura, and naturally irritated by his jealousy; Laura, for once out in society, and delighted in a very happy and excited way (no touch of the coquette, though, about the future Mrs Pendennis); and Blanche, showing off but rather eclipsed by Laura :

> Miss Blanche was, indeed, the *vis-à-vis* of Miss Laura, and smiled most killingly upon her dearest friend, and nodded to her, and talked to her, when they met during the quadrille evolutions, and patronized her a great deal. Her shoulders were the whitest in the whole room : and they were never easy in her frock for one single instant : nor were her eyes, which rolled about incessantly : nor was her little figure :– it seemed to say to all the people, 'Come and look at me – not at that pink, healthy, bouncing country lass, Miss Bell, who scarcely knew how to dance till I taught her. This is the true Parisian manner – this is the prettiest little foot in the room, and the prettiest little *chaussure*, too.'
> (Chap. 26)

Thackeray brings out the competitiveness and the troubles of balls, not omitting the small but real horrors of getting a bad partner. He punishes Blanche by making her dance with Captain Broadfoot of the Dragoons, an unlucky dancer who 'though devoting himself with great energy to the object in view, could not get round in time : and, not having the least ear for music, was unaware that his movements were too slow'.

Thackeray's farce (like his dramatic discoveries) contributes to the psychological drama and he shows Pen, encouraged first by jealousy and then by 'mischief', refusing to dance with Laura, and recklessly enjoying himself, as quiz, wit and satirist. Here Pen is like Becky, another example of the satirist's satire of satirists. The ball provides Pen with good materials, as the Pitt household did for Becky's amusing letter :

> Pen was delighted with his mischief. The two prettiest girls in the room were quarrelling about him. He flattered himself he had punished Miss Laura. He leaned in a dandified air, with his elbow over the wall, and talked to Blanche. He quizzed unmercifully all the men in the room – the heavy Dragoons in their tight jackets – the country dandies in their queer attire – the strange toilettes of the ladies. One seemed to have a bird's nest in her hair; another had six pounds of grapes in her hair, besides her false pearls. 'It's a *coiffure* of almonds and raisins,' said Pen, 'and might be served up for dessert.' In a word, Pen was exceedingly satirical and amusing. (Ibid.)

Thackeray is always good at showing the headiness of festivity, even where it is not the result of ordinary intoxication, but of dancing, competitiveness, a licensed public display. It is not just Pen's pride and conceit, but the full-dress festive version of his working-day qualities, that are shown as coming before his fall :

> And now taking his time, and with his fair partner Blanche hanging lovingly on the arm which encircled her, Mr Arthur Pendennis set out upon his waltzing career, and felt, as he whirled round to the music, that he and Blanche were performing very brilliantly indeed. Very likely he looked to see if Miss Bell thought so too; but she did not or would not see him, and was always engaged with her partner Captain Strong. But Pen's triumph was not destined to last long : and it was doomed that poor Blanche was to have yet another discomfiture on that unfortunate night. While she and Pen were whirling round as light and brisk as a couple of opera-dancers, honest Captain Broadfoot and the lady round whose large waist he was clinging,

were twisting round very leisurely according to their natures, and indeed were in everybody's way. But they were more in Pendennis's way than in anybody's else, for he and Blanche, whilst executing their rapid gyrations, came bolt up against the heavy Dragoon and his lady, and with such force that the centre of gravity was lost by all four of the circumvolving bodies; Captain Broadfoot and Miss Roundle were fairly upset, as was Pen himself, who was less lucky than his partner Miss Amory, who was only thrown upon a bench against a wall.

But Pendennis came fairly down upon the floor, sprawling in the general ruin with Broadfoot and Miss Roundle. The captain, though heavy, was good-natured, and was the first to burst out into a loud laugh at his own misfortune, which nobody therefore heeded. But Miss Amory was savage at her mishap. Miss Roundel, placed on her *séant*, and looking pitifully round, presented an object which very few people could see without laughing; and Pen was furious when he heard the people giggling about him. He was one of those sarcastic young fellows that did not bear a laugh at his own expense, and of all things in the world feared ridicule most. (Ibid.)

Thackeray is not content with one fall in this scene, and he goes on to make Pen blunder so in his apologies to Blanche that 'in a pet' she accepts a glass of water and the arm of the nearest man (misleadingly wearing a 'blue ribbon and a three-pointed star') and goes off to dance with him while Pen, forgetting 'humiliation in his surprise', cries out, 'By Jove, it's the cook!' Thackeray enjoys the socially promiscuous occasion here, not only in order to punish Blanche with more farce, but in order to make his unobtrusive social comments. He does not need to tell us how susceptible his young women are to ribbons and stars; and quietly lets Blanche 'assume' that Mirobolant is some foreign nobleman, having 'never fairly looked in the artist's face since he had been employed in her mother's family'. Strong tells Mirobolant, in Spanish, that he cannot walk with Blanche, and this scene too moves from waltzing to brawling, another low-life crowd gathers outside the windows to cheer and jeer. But Pen behaves decently to the injured chef, and the scene ends with the tiny detail of Blanche 'as pale as a lemon-ice' looking rather upset because she has met a mysterious man who knew her father. The scene is important in the plotting, but since the plot itself is by far the less interesting part of the novel, especially in these later chapters, the scene is chiefly valuable as comedy of manners and of character.

In its pattern of rise-and-fall and social confusion, it is placed in the larger pattern. There is another important scene of festive *contretemps*, also important in the plot, when 'The Sylph Reappears'. This takes place in one of the many marvellous dining-rooms in Thackeray, described in a set-piece as good as the description of the Newcomes' house :

. . . They admired the dining-room with fitting compliments, and pronounced it 'very chaste,' – that being the proper phrase. There were, indeed, high-backed Dutch chairs of the seventeenth century; there was a sculptured carved buffet of the sixteenth; there was a sideboard robbed out of the carved work of a church in the Low Countries, and a large brass cathedral lamp over the round oak table; there were old family portraits from Wardour Street and tapestry from France, bits of armour, double-handed swords and battle-axes made of *carton-pierre*, looking-glasses, statuettes of saints, and Dresden china – nothing, in a word, could be chaster. Behind the dining-room was the library, fitted with busts and books all of a size, and wonderful easy-chairs, and solemn bronzes in the severe classic style. Here it was that, guarded by double doors, Sir Francis smoked cigars, and read *Bell's Life in London*, and went to sleep after dinner, when he was not smoking over the billiard-table at his clubs, or punting at the gambling-houses in St James's.

But what could equal the chaste splendour of the drawing-rooms? – the carpets were so magnificently fluffy that your foot made no more noise on them than your shadow : on their white ground bloomed roses and tulips as big as warming-pans : about the room were high chairs and low chairs, bandy-legged chairs, chairs so attenuated that it was a wonder any but a sylph could sit upon them, marqueterie-tables covered with marvellous gimcracks, china ornaments of all ages and countries, bronzes, gilt daggers, Books of Beauty, yataghans, Turkish papooshes, and boxes of Parisian bonbons. Wherever you sate down there were Dresden shepherds and shepherdesses convenient at your elbow; there were, moreover, light blue poodles and ducks and cocks and hens in porcelain; there were nymphs by Boucher, and shepherdesses by Greuze, very chaste indeed; there were muslin curtains and brocade curtains, gilt cages with parroquets and love-birds, two squealing cockatoos, each out-squealing and out-chattering the other; a clock singing tunes on a console-table, and another booming the hours like Great Tom, on the mantelpiece – there was, in a word, everything that comfort could desire, and the most elegant taste devise. A London drawing-room fitted up without regard to expense, is surely one of the noblest and most curious sights of the present day. The Romans of the Lower Empire, the dear Marchionesses and Countesses of Louis XV, could scarcely have had a finer taste than our modern folks exhibit; and everybody who saw Lady Clavering's reception-rooms was forced to confess that they were most elegant; and that the prettiest rooms in London – Lady Harley Quin's, Lady Hanway Wardour's, or Mrs Hodge-Podgson's own, the great Railroad Croesus's wife, were not fitted up with a more consummate 'chastity'.

Poor Lady Clavering, meanwhile, knew little regarding these things, and had a sad want of respect for the splendours around her. 'I only know they cost a precious deal of money, major,' she said to her guest, 'and that I don't advise you to try one of them gossamer gilt chairs : *I* came down on one the night we gave our second dinner-party. Why didn't you come and see us before? We'd have asked you to it.'

'You would have liked to see mamma break a chair. . . .'

(Chap. 37)

Here the conspicuous objects form not only a display of expensive bad taste, backed with the usual information about the source of the money, but play their part in the motif of the comic fall. The scenery also prepares for the big scene in the next chapter, 'In Which Captain Altamont Appears and Disappears', which begins with some more promising class-detail :

. . . The major looked very sulkily at Strong, being by no means well pleased to sit down to dinner with Clavering's d— house-steward. . . . But Mr Welbore Welbore . . . speedily arriving, Pendennis the elder was somewhat appeased, for Welbore, though perfectly dull, and taking no more part in the conversation at dinner than the footman behind his chair, was a respectable country gentleman of ancient family and seven thousand a year; and the major felt always at ease in such society. (Chap. 38)

The disruption of this feast takes place when the ladies have left the gentlemen to their wine, and it is important in the plot, because Altamont looks into the gorgeous dining-room, himself just as gorgeous, 'his copious black hair was evidently surreptitious, and his whiskers of the Tyrian purple' and 'attired with chains, jewellery, and waistcoats, which the illumination of the house lighted up to great advantage'. The brawl, involving the usual 'low-life' crowd, a footman and the police, is introduced because it gives Major Pendennis some very valuable information about the skeleton in the Claverings' cupboard and permits the real temptation of Pen to begin. The incident is an excellent example of Thackeray's comic powers as he describes the split set, the dining-room visible to the street, and the street-scene itself, with little boys jumping up and down, looking at the 'six gentlemen in white waistcoats', saying, 'Mi hi, Jim, shouldn't you like to be there, and have a cut of that there pineapple', horses and carriages passing by, conveying the nobility and gentry 'to Belgravian toilets', and policemen patrolling up and down :

> . . . The gasman came and lighted the lamps before Sir Francis's door; the butler entered the dining-room, and illuminated the antique gothic chandelier over the antique dining-table : so that from outside the house you looked inwards upon a night scene of feasting and wax candles; and from within you beheld a vision of a calm summer evening, and the wall of St James's Park, and the sky above, in which a star or two was just beginning to twinkle. (Ibid.)

The scene is full of quiet humour, social information, and a display of expensive objects, furniture, clothes, food, drink and service. Mrs Gaskell and Dickens use this kind of detailed social contrast to make a direct appeal to the sense of justice (particularly in *Mary Barton* and *Bleak House*), but Thackeray's method is one of quiet implicitness in which description does the work. Even the little poor London boys are entirely amusing, not pathetic.

The rise-and-fall of ceremony is characterized in many other comic scenes which work similarly, if less climactically. There are for instance, all the feasts at Oxbridge, including the very splendid dinner-party which Major Pendennis thinks is a special occasion, but which, alas for Pen's patrimony, is nothing out of

the way in this 'Rake's Progress'.[8] There are the disreputable
merry meetings at the Back Kitchen, where Pen renews acquaintance with Costigan, and where there is usually enjoyment and
companionship. There are a few more honest and simple meals,
some with Warrington, who on one occasion offers to grill a
chop for the Major. There is the eloquent indoor pastoral, where
Thackeray shows the snobbish shamed response of Wagg as guest
and Pen as host when Betsy staggers in with a tray of tea and
thick bread and butter for an everyday inelegant repast. It
would be misleading to say that Thackeray uses this kind of
contrast often. His method is to present scenes of high living so
that they speak for themselves. Meals, dining-rooms, guests, conversation, music, drink, dance, occur, page after page, in
Vauxhall, in St James's, in Belgravia, in the country, in great
houses, in the houses of the *nouveaux riches*, in Bohemian Grub
Street. There is nearly always a failure of ceremony and of
fellowship.

Both in *Pendennis* and in *The Newcomes* Thackeray satirizes
the festive life of intellectual London, either through the lion-
hunting and tuft-hunting which give names to several of his
comic hostesses, or through scenes which show the writers and
artists in their own haunts, usually poor, and usually with a rich
social and cultural mixture. The novels tell the story of society
but also of individuals, and, as has been emphasized, their
picture of manners is a stage designed to show the fortunes of a
Becky, a Pendennis or a Clive Newcome. In *Pendennis* Thackeray is interested in a Snob's Progress much more precisely, I
think, than Dickens was to be in *Great Expectations*, even though
Pen never commits himself as permanently or as single-mindedly
to snobbery as Pip.

The relationship between Dickens and Thackeray is a complex
and fascinating one. They read each other's novels anxiously
and responsively. Thackeray suggested on one occasion, pleasantly
and quite modestly, that what he saw as a more natural style in
David Copperfield might have been a result of his reading *Vanity
Fair*. On the other hand, *Esmond* is very likely to be a response
to Dickens's first-person success in *David Copperfield*. It is
possible that *Great Expectations* owes much, consciously or not,

[8] This is the title of Chap. 19.

to *Pendennis*, in the presentation of a sensitive man's susceptibility to pomp and ceremony. From an early date both writers –
Dickens in *Pickwick* and Thackeray in *The Book of Snobs* –
dramatize and analyse the vanities of food, and the snobbishness
of party-giving and dining out; but what seems more definitely
to link Pendennis and Pip is the very close analytic contrast of
simple and generous hospitality with elegant and hollow show
or sham. Both novelists are interested in the responses and
behaviour (for which we have no one descriptive word) of the
guest, and certainly a part of Thackeray's purpose, whether or
not it instructed Dickens, was to show Pendennis as a guest
tempted by snobbishness, but not falling. While being educated
in worldliness by Major Pendennis, he has to dine in Grub
Street where he does not always please his hosts or fellow-guests.
But Thackeray shows Pen with other snobs. The best literary
festivity showing 'The Dining-Out Snob'[9] is the 'Dinner in the
Row' where Pen dines with his publisher, in a beautiful scene
of cultural promiscuity. The guests include a lord's son, Wagg
and Wenham the snobs, and various successful, struggling and
eccentric writers, including the literary lady Miss Bunion. In
Pendennis, but not in *Mrs Perkin's Ball* where she also appears,
she is a fine example of Thackeray's charitable humour, as he
distinguishes it both in theory and performance, from the un-
charitable wit and satire that always characterize Becky and
sometimes Pen :

> Pen, who had read, and rather admired some of her works
> (and expected to find in Miss Bunion a person somewhat
> resembling her own description of herself in the *Passion-Flower*,
> in which she stated that her youth resembled –

> > A violet, shrinking meanly
> > When blows the March wind keenly;
> > A timid fawn, on wild-wood lawn,
> > Where oak-boughs rustle greenly, –

> and that her maturer beauty was something very different,
> certainly, to the artless loveliness of her prime, but still exceed-
> ingly captivating, and striking), beheld, rather to his surprise and
> amusement, a large and bony woman in a crumpled satin dress,
> who came creaking into the room with a step as heavy as a

[9] One of the essay-titles in *The Book of Snobs*.

grenadier's. Wagg instantly noted the straw which she brought in at the rumpled skirt of her dress, and would have stooped to pick it up; but Miss Bunion disarmed all criticism by observing this ornament herself, and, putting her own large foot upon it, so as to separate it from her robe, she stopped and picked up the straw, saying to Mrs Bungay, that she was very sorry to be a little late, but that the omnibus was very slow, and what a comfort it was to get a ride all the way from Brompton for sixpence. Nobody laughed at the poetess's speech, it was uttered so simply. Indeed, the worthy woman had not the least notion of being ashamed of an action incidental upon her poverty.

(Chap. 34)

As usual, it is a scene packed with sociological information. Mrs Bungay, the hostess, is 'evidently' preoccupied with extraneous thoughts as she greets her guests, disturbed by her dinner-party, as the grander hosts and hostesses in Thackeray do not need to be.[10] We are told about the transport, carriage with job-horses instead of hack-cabs; about the literary professions and ranks, Mr Bole, the real editor of the magazine of which Mr Wagg was the nominal chief; Mr Trotter, who 'from having broken out on the world as a poet of a tragic and suicidal cast, had now subsided into one of Mr Bungay's back shops as reader for that gentleman; and Captain Sumph, an ex-beau, still about town, and related in some indistinct manner to Literature and the Peerage', said to have written a book and given to anecdotes of Byron and recollections of Shelley, on which he dines out.

As usual, attention is paid to the 'sham grandeur', of the 'sham butler' who is 'an undertaker in Amen Corner' and the 'sham wine'. The critic here is a sham guest, as Thackeray shows obliquely :

He's the sham butler here; and I observe, my dear Mr. Pendennis, as you will through life, that wherever there is a sham butler at a London dinner there is sham wine – this sherry is filthy. Bungay, my boy, where did you get this delicious brown sherry?'

The conversation has a splendid range. Miss Bunion does not take to Pen, who is attired so fashionably and gives himself such grand airs that she takes him 'for one of the little Mayfair

---

[10] This detail and many similar ones originate in *The Book of Snobs*.

dandies' and sensibly decides to 'eat my dinner and hold my tongue', as she tells Pen on a later occasion when she has decided that he is not as solemn, stupid or pert as he looks. Wagg makes unpleasant remarks to Pen and pleasant ones to his host and hostess. The hostess is disturbed by Wagg's French '*brimborion à la Sevigné*' and Popjoy's '*cordon bleu*' which she not unreasonably takes to be probably a 'jack-chain'. Wagg whispers about the origin and price of the food, and recalls Mrs Rawdon Crawley's parties, where the champagne was always so good, coming from Gaunt House with the butler. There is the perennial conversation of many literary parties, not so much about literature as about the literature business. Shandon, more brilliant than Wagg, does not shine, subdued by the wit 'of the more successful man', and by his wife who watches his glass. Wagg tells how Popjoy's novel was based on an old magazine story; Sumph tells how he remembers 'poor Byron, Hobhouse, Trelawney, and myself, dining with Cardinal Mezzocaldo' and drinking Orvieto; Shandon suggests that Sumph publish his stories, and then goes on to a discussion of the proposed new magazine, the *Pall Mall Gazette*.[11]

More successful than many of the other dinner-parties in the novel, its criticism of society is made not by a single grand *contretemps*, but by many little ones, as well as by the self-damning flow of compliment and criticism. The satire is not snobbish; Thackeray treats the inelegant hostess and the clumsy Miss Bunion with respect and affection, preserving his satire, as in *Vanity Fair*, for performances, greed and hypocrisy that are more dangerous than sham wine and sham butlers.

In *The Newcomes*, novel of the *nouveaux riches*, the comic feasts are all marked by precariousness, though the other themes are present too, sham hospitality, sham politeness, social mixture, confusion, vicious sensuality, and acquisitiveness. Triviality is often emphasized, not just as a waste of time, but as a bad substitute for friendliness and real human relations, as in this ball scene :

---

[11] The real *Pall Mall Gazette*, which started in 1865, was named after the fictional magazine in *Pendennis*, as a compliment to Thackeray.

'Do you know many people? This is your first appearance in society? Shall I introduce you to some nice girls to dance with? What very pretty buttons!'

'Is that what you wanted to say?' asked Clive, rather bewildered.

'What does one say at a ball? One talks conversation suited to the place. If I were to say to Captain Crackthorpe, "What pretty buttons" he would be delighted. But you – you have a soul above buttons, I suppose.'

'Being as you say, a stranger in this sort of society, you see I am not accustomed to – to the exceeding brilliancy of its conversation,' said Clive. (Chap. 61)

In the early scenes where Colonel Newcome brings Clive to the Back Kitchen and joins in the singing, and is furious when Costigan disturbs the censorship which has been introduced for Clive's sake (*maxima pueris debetur*, Thackeray often says), there is a disturbance of ceremony, as there is also in a later scene in Miss Honeyman's Brighton when the Marquis of Farintosh and Clive are fellow-guests, each speaking his own jealous language. There is the expensive and rather rowdy party at the Star and Garter, Richmond (also patronized by Lord Steyne and Major Pendennis), where Farintosh says farewell to his days of philandering – a brilliant example of Thackeray's powers of dramatic summary. 'The Dinner in the Row' or 'Contains Some Ball-Practising' were long, elaborate, detailed, various, but Thackeray is also master of the brief but animated summary:

We all know in what an affecting farewell he took leave of the associates of his *vie de garcon*: the speeches made (in both languages), the presents distributed, the tears and hysterics of some of the guests assembled; the cigar-boxes given over to this friend, the *écrin* of diamonds to that, et cætera, et cætera, et cætera. . . . The farewell at Greenwich was so affecting that all 'traversed the cart', and took another farewell at Richmond, where there was crying too, but it was Eucharis cried because fair Calypso wanted to tear her eyes out; and where not only Telemachus (as was natural to his age), but Mentor likewise, quaffed the wine-cup too freely. You are virtuous, O reader! but there are still cakes and ale. (Chap. 59)

There are also some scenes of festivity which break up in

similar disarray, but are used more climactically for the purpose of developing plot and relationship; such as the dinner-party in Chapter 13 where Clive throws the claret at Barnes, the ball at Baden which has a more serious version of the rudely disrupted dancing in *Pendennis* and ends in a duel. The acquisitiveness that marks many feasts is emphasized implicitly and scarcely mentioned, left to speak for itself. When Clive returns to England from Italy after his father's Bundelcund Banking Company has begun to do so very well, he mentions ingenuously to Pendennis that everyone has been very kind and welcoming,

even Barnes. There follow a number of dinner-parties, some summarized, some dramatized in detail, that insist on this ulterior acquisitive motive. These scenes are splendid illustrations of interested, axe-grinding social mixtures. There is not only mixture of classes, however, but of people brought together without fellowship in a spurious show of harmony, people who not only have nothing to say to each other but who in some cases rather dislike each other. Aggression and competition are often close to the surface. The sham here is a criticism of the moneyed society.

In Chapter 68, for instance, Barnes is behaving as the perfect host, Lord Highgate paying incessant and deceptive attention to Ethel, Clive scowling in furious jealousy, Lady Clara silent. There is one empty seat, intended for but not occupied by the Marquis of Farintosh who, as so often, in party after party, during his pursuit by Lady Kew and Ethel, is invited but does not come. In the same chapter some of Pendennis's narration of the social surface probes beneath the surface. Pendennis tells how Barnes is kind to everyone, from his pimply young cousin, to whom he talks about King's College, thereby knocking over 'not only Sam but his mamma too', to Uncle Hobson about crops, Clive about his pictures, Pendennis about the political effect of an article in the *Pall Mall Gazette*. We get a strong ironic picture of what Barnes is after, and why he gives dinners. We gather still more in the next chapter, pointedly called 'Contains at Least Six More Courses and Two Desserts', which provides a realistic domestic post-mortem after the party. Thackeray drops the narrative form, and as on several occasions in *The Newcomes* brilliantly and subtly uses dramatic dialogue. Pendennis as narrator is redundant here, and it is his wife who reinterprets the scene. Sometimes she hints meaningfully: 'Lord Highgate was very attentive to Miss Newcome, was he?' Sometimes she says nothing, as when Pendennis says, 'And now he is off with the old love, Laura, and on with the new. Why do you look at me so? Are you thinking that other people have been in love two or three times too?' To which she replies, 'I am thinking that I should not like to live in London, Arthur.' At times she says something explicit, as when she tells how Barnes, 'that dreary, languid, pale, bald, cadaverous leering man' whispered 'what they call gallantry' to her.

On several other occasions the clandestine nature of the entertainments – or the opportunity given to the clandestine relationship – is brought out, with suitable reticence, as Pendennis gradually comes to see what is going on beneath the surface. Ethel, Clive, the Pendennises, Barnes, his wife, Lord Highgate, the Marquis of Farintosh and Lady Kew, sometimes other members of the Newcome family, continually play in shifting permutations the game of unhappy families. Dining out becomes an important scenic and verbal vehicle in the development of the twin actions with a single theme, Lord Highgate's pursuit of Clara, victim of the marriage-market, and Ethel's

pursuit of Farintosh, which could end by victimizing both of
them. The drama also analyses and exposes the social oppor-
tunities which weave such webs. The hospitality is not just a
meaningless game, but a trap. Hosts invite their clients, people
who may be useful or influential. It is such a familiar pattern
that there is scarcely any need to invoke Veblen :

> As wealth accumulates on his hands, his own unaided effort will
> not avail to sufficiently put his opulence in evidence. . . . The aid
> of friends and competitors is therefore brought in by resorting
> to the giving of valuable presents and expensive feasts and
> entertainments. . . . The competitor with whom the entertainer
> wishes to institute a comparison is, by this method, made to serve
> as a means to the end. He consumes vicariously for his host at
> the same time that he is a witness to the consumption of that
> excess of good things which his host is unable to dispose of
> single-handed, and he is also made to witness his host's facility
> in etiquette. (Op. cit., Chap. 4)

These Newcome feasts are also business enterprises, designed
to enlist, secure, and impress clients. This commercial aspect was
also present in the literary dinners in *Pendennis,* for which there
is, interestingly, no equivalent in' the world of art dramatized in
The Newcomes. It is most strongly presented in the rich entertainments given by Colonel Newcome, after the Bundelcund
Bank has begun to rise and also after it has begun to fall.
Thackeray again combines social satire, plot tension, and the
portrait of a good man, tainted slightly, by ambition and
acquisitiveness. All Colonel Newcome really wanted was money
to buy Ethel for Clive, or, to put it another way, to allow Clive
to enter the competition for Ethel. He is sufficiently of the world
to know that money will be needed, and Barnes's greed confirms
this, but he is too innocent to realize that Lady Kew, being
particularly greedy, wants rank as well as money. (Interestingly
like and unlike Lord Steyne, her brother, showing the same ruthlessness, good taste, predatoriness and sensuality, Lady Kew is
placed in a more precarious position, as a member of the
aristocracy necessarily allied to those gentry who have started
to marry into the monied middle classes.) Colonel Newcome is
shown, in a large-scale act of loving present-giving, as attempting
to play the marriage-market for the best reasons. But the result

is a certain contamination; when he cannot buy Ethel, his mind turns to Rosey, and the result is Clive's disastrous marriage. In many ways Colonel Newcome continues to behave nobly, and does not sell out, for instance, when the shares begin to fall. His hostility to Ethel is understandable, but combined with his growing pleasure in money and power and his ostentatious entertainments, it makes him an altogether less sympathetic character than the old, easy, generous Colonel Newcome who began the novel. His feasts are comic and weary, marked with ennui, composed of people who are brought together only by a financial interest :

I confess that a dinner at the colonel's, now he appeared in all his magnificence, was awfully slow. No peaches could look fresher that Rosey's cheeks, – no damask was fairer than her pretty little shoulders. No one, I am sure, could be happier than she, but she did not impart her happiness to her friends; and replied chiefly by smiles to the conversation of the gentlemen at her side. It is true that these were for the most part elderly dignitaries, distinguished military officers with blue-black whiskers, retired old Indian judges, and the like, occupied with their victuals, and generally careless to please. But that solemn happiness of the colonel, who shall depict it : – that look of affection with which he greeted his daughter as she entered, flounced to the waist, twinkling with innumerable jewels, holding a dainty pocket-handkerchief, with smiling eyes, dimpled cheeks, and golden ringlets! He would take her hand, or follow her about from group to group, exchanging precious observations about the weather, the Park, the Exhibition, nay, the Opera, for the old man actually went to the Opera with his little girl, and solemnly snoozed by her side in a white waistcoat. (Chap. 62)

Most important, they are precarious. In that last extract, the skeleton at the feast is replaced by the bizarre, ponderous and emblematic object, the coco-nut tree.[12] On its very first appearance it showed the sinister omission of Hobson Newcome's name from the list of subscribers to the Bank which were 'engraven on the trunk of Mr Newcome's allegorical silver coco-nut-tree', as

---

[12] Jean Sudrann has some fine observations on this object in her article, ' "The Philosopher's Property" : Thackeray and the Use of Time', op. cit. (Introduction n. 6).

Fred Bayham points out in Chapter 64, which is called 'Absit Omen'. The coco-nut tree unites three social symbols: the sinister present, the expensive object, and the rich feast, for the tree is as useful as it is ornamental, having 'leaves dexterously arranged for holding candles and pickles'. It is also historically eloquent as a representative art object, being at the same time a memorial to the elaboration of Victorian design and to the far-flung Empire. It is a miniature and parody of the intricacy and imperial symbolism of the Albert Memorial. It is worth looking at in detail :

> There was a superb silver coco-nut-tree, whereof the leaves were dexterously arranged for holding candles and pickles; under the coco-nut was an Indian prince on a camel giving his hand to a cavalry officer on horseback – a howitzer, a plough, a loom, a bale of cotton, on which were the East India Company's arms, a brahmin, Britannia, and Commerce, with a cornucopia were grouped round the principal figures : and if you would see a noble account of this chaste and elegant specimen of British art, you are referred to the pages of the *Pall Mall Gazette* of that year, as well as to Fred Bayham's noble speech in the course of the evening, when it was exhibited. The East and its wars, and its heroes, Assaye and Seringapatam ('and Lord Lake and Laswaree too', calls out the colonel greatly elated) tiger-hunting palanquins, Juggernaut, elephants, the burning of widows – all passed before us in F.B.'s splendid oration. He spoke of the product of the Indian forest, the palm-tree, the coco-nut-tree, the banyan-tree. Palms the colonel had already brought back with him, the palms of valour, won in the field of war (cheers). Coco-nut-trees he had never seen, though he had heard wonders related regarding the milky contents of their fruit. Here at any rate was one tree of the kind, under the branches of which he humbly trusted often to repose – and, if he might be so bold as to carry on the Eastern metaphor, he would say, knowing the excellence of the colonel's claret and the splendour of his hospitality, that he would prefer a coco-nut day at the colonel's to a banyan day anywhere else. Whilst F.B.'s speech went on, I remember J.J. eyeing the trophy, and the queer expression of his shrewd face. The health of British Artists was drunk à propos of this splendid specimen of their skill. . . . (Chap. 63)

The coco-nut tree is not only a comic Victorian ornament, tribute to art and industry, like the multiple-bladed knife exhibited in the 1851 exhibition, which can still be seen in the window of John Weiss & Son Ltd, Wigmore Street, London. It is also, in its unJamesian way, the golden bowl of this novel, appearing from time to time to make ominous signals, intended as a present and turning out to be a curse. Some of its signatories, it is remarked, sell out. It also signals the desperate and prudent keeping up of appearances, for later feasts at the Newcomes' splendid residences are essential if futile gestures in an attempt at keeping up faith in the B.B.C. Sometimes its absence expresses an informal and pastoral relaxation and enjoyment, as in Chapter 66, though even in this relatively friendly and easy gathering Clive is the skeleton and the outsider, moodily biting his nails. On later occasions, there is ennui, gloom, heaviness and the sense of social change, which Thackeray is very good at chronicling, over small and large periods of time :

> I myself dined once or twice with my old friends, under the shadow of the pickle-bearing coco-nut-tree; and could not but remark a change of personages in the society assembled. The manager of the city branch of the B.B.C. was always present – an ominous-looking man, whose whispers and compliments seemed to make poor Clive, at his end of the table, very melancholy. With the city manager came the city manager's friends, whose jokes passed gaily round, and who kept the conversation to themselves. Once I had the happiness to meet Mr Ratray, who had returned, filled with rupees from the Indian bank; who told us many anecdotes of the splendour of Rummun Loll at Calcutta, who complimented the colonel on his fine house and grand dinners with sinister good humour. Those compliments did not seem to please our poor friend; that familiarity choked him. A brisk little chattering attorney, very intimate with Sherrick, with a wife of dubious gentility, was another constant guest. . . . Where were the generals and the judges? Where were the fogies and their respectable ladies? Stupid they were, and dull their company, but better a stalled ox in their society, than Mr Campion's jokes over Mr Sherrick's wines.
> (Chap. 70)

This most conspicuously Victorian article makes its last appearance in the text as a sad relic in the box of loot Mrs

'TO BE SOLD'

Mackenzie tries to salvage from the wreck.[13] Thereafter the
Colonel ceases to be the host and becomes the poor relation and
unwanted guest. The feasts are replaced by unceremonious meals
and meetings, where poverty and family hostility, meanness and
resentment join together. There are still telling details of what
was eaten and drunk, such as the cold beef which was all they
had to offer Pendennis, and which Mrs Mackenzie inspects
suspiciously for signs of erosion by the servants; or the pâté with
which she hypocritically and greedily entertains Pendennis when
he visits them in Boulogne. The splendour of the Newcomes is
not contrasted so much with pastoral peace and harmony (there is
some of this in the Pendennis domestic chorus) as with hostility
without the covers and consolations of festivity. It ceases to be
comic and weary and becomes merely weary.

Some of the most vicious festivities appear in *The Virginians*,
the sequel to *Esmond*. The specialized theme in these feasts is
hospitality, almost entirely shown in the negative, but working
initially through a somewhat deceptive pastoral contrast between
the hospitality of England and America. In the English feasts,
there is a strong emphasis on the *memento mori* :

Mrs B.'s closets, for what you know, are stuffed with skeletons.
Look there under the sofa-cushion. Is that merely missy's doll,
or is it the limb of a stifled Cupid peeping out? What do you
suppose are those ashes smouldering in the grate? – Very likely
a suttee has been offered up there just before you came in : a
faithful heart has been burned out upon a callous corpse, and
you are looking on the *cineri doloso*. You see B. and his wife
receiving their company before dinner. Gracious powers! Do
you know that that bouquet which she wears is a signal to
Captain C., and that he will find a note under the little bronze
Shakespeare on the mantelpiece in the study? And with all this
you go up and say some uncommonly neat thing (as you fancy)
to Mrs B. about the weather (clever dog!), or about Lady E.'s
last party (fashionable buck!), or about the dear children in the
nursery (insinuating rogue!). Heaven and earth, my good sir,
how can you tell that B. is not going to pitch all the children
out of the nursery window this very night, or that his lady has

[13] In the first and subsequent illustrated editions of *The Newcomes*, the
coco-nut tree reappears in Richard Doyle's sketch of the auction of Colonel
Newcome's effects, which is included in the present volume (see opposite).

not made an arrangement for leaving them, and running off
with the captain? How do you know that those footmen are
not disguised bailiffs? – that yonder large-looking butler (really
a skeleton) is not the pawnbroker's man? and that there are not
skeleton *rôtis* and entrées under every one of the covers? Look
at their feet peeping from under the tablecloth. Mind how you
stretch out your own lovely little slippers, madam, lest you knock
over a rib or two. Remark the Death's-head moths fluttering
among the flowers. See the pale winding-sheets gleaming in the
wax-candles! I know it is an old story, and especially that this
preacher has yelled *vanitas vanitatum* five hundred times before.
(Chap. 26)

The precariousness and discord mark these feasts, and the
theme of false appearances is also visible from the beginning in
the innocent expectations of Harry Warrington, Thackeray's
only 'cheerful' hero, who comes expecting welcome from the
Castlewoods, but finds instead the cold comfort of an inn, then
a rude, reluctant welcome from his cousins, and last a predatory
and spurious hospitality :

At present he but saw that his kinsfolks received him not unkindly.
Lady Castlewood was perfectly civil to him; the young ladies
pleasant and pleased; my Lord Castlewood, a man of cold and
haughty demeanour, was not more reserved towards Harry than
to any of the rest of the family; Mr William was ready to drink
with him, to ride with him, to go to races with him, and to play
cards with him. When he proposed to go away, they one and all
pressed him to stay. Madame de Bernstein did not tell him
how it arose that he was the object of such eager hospitality. He
did not know what schemes he was serving or disarranging,
whose or what anger he was creating. He fancied he was welcome
because those around him were his kinsmen, and never thought
that those could be his enemies out of whose cup he was drinking,
and whose hand he was pressing every night and morning.
(Chap. 14)

He soon comes to see the solicitation in the welcome, and makes
his opinion clear. His lady cousins want to dance and flirt,
because he is thought to be a rich heir; his cousin Will and the
chaplain engage him in play, and he shows that he has a dry
wit, despite his ingenuousness, as he comments : 'I'm used to make

my own bets upon my own judgment, and don't need any
relations to select them for me, thank you. But as I am your
guest, and no doubt, you want to show me hospitality, I'll take
your bet – there. And so Done and Done.' Not only do they try
to make money out of him by gambling, but give unfair odds
and cheat him of a horse. Just as Thackeray criticizes the worldly
feast but has a special tart word to say for the sham quality, so
he criticizes play and also unfair play, and with the full weight
of personal experience. In *Vanity Fair* he seems to suggest that
between different forms of play there is little to choose, in the
superb comment, 'If we play, let it be with clean cards'. (Chap.
64) Occasionally in *The Virginians* Thackeray creates a scene
which is a masterpiece of deadpan satire :

> In this easy manner the Sabbath day passed. The evening was
> beautiful, and there was talk of adjourning to a cool tankard
> and a game of whist in a summer-house; but the company voted
> to sit indoors, the ladies declaring they thought the aspect of
> three honours in their hand, and some good court cards, more
> beautiful than the loveliest scene of nature; and so the sun went
> behind the elms, and still they were at their cards; and the rooks
> came home cawing their even song, and they never stirred except
> to change partners; and the chapel clock tolled hour after hour
> unheeded, so delightfully were they spent over the pasteboard;
> and the moon and stars came out; and it was nine o'clock, and
> the groom of the chambers announced that supper was ready.
>
> (Chap. 15)

Here the calm opposition of nature and play makes the point
without fuss, even the mention of the Sabbath making its
presence felt in a very subdued irony. Thackeray was no sab-
batarian, but here the 'Sabbath' makes its rebuke, a rebuke
dependent on the context of the whole novel, which criticizes
English aristocratic vanity. It makes the criticism partly by
comparisons with the simple life of the Lamberts, home cooking,[14]
real family affection and domestic virtues, and partly by the
contrast with America :

> 'I mean, cousin, that we of the Virginian house owe you

[14] Thackeray almost tolerantly brings out the solicitation in Mrs Lambert's
praise of her daughter's cooking.

nothing but our own,' continued Harry Warrington; 'but our own, and the hospitality which you are now showing me.'

'You are heartily welcome to both. You were hurt by the betting just now?'

'Well,' replied the lad, 'I am sort o' hurt. Your welcome, you see, is different to our welcome, and that's the fact. At home we are glad to see a man, hold out a hand to him, and give him of our best. Here you take us in, give us beef and claret enough, to be sure, and don't seem to care when we come, or when we go. That's the remark which I have been making, since I have been in your lordship's house; I can't help telling it out, you see, now 'tis on my mind; and I think I am a little easier now I have said it.' (Ibid.)

But this is Harry's point, not Thackeray's, and he soon follows it with the confidential comment that there are criticisms to be made even of Virginian hospitality :

When Harry gave to Lord Castlewood those flourishing descriptions of the maternal estate in America, he had not wished to mislead his kinsman, or to boast, or to tell falsehoods, for the lad was of a very honest and truth-telling nature; but, in his life at home, it must be owned that the young fellow had had acquaintance with all sorts of queer company, – horse-jockeys, tavern loungers, gambling and sporting men, of whom a great number were found in his native colony. A landed aristocracy with a population of negroes to work their fields, and cultivate their tobacco and corn, had little other way of amusement than in the hunting-field, or over the cards and the punch-bowl. The hospitality of the province was unbounded : every man's house was his neighbour's; and the idle gentlefolks rode from one mansion to another, finding in each pretty much the same sport – welcome, and rough plenty. The Virginian squire had often a bare-footed valet, and a cobbled saddle; but there was plenty of corn for the horses, and abundance of drink and venison for the master within the tumbledown fences, and behind the cracked windows of the hall. Harry had slept on many a straw mattress, and engaged in endless jolly night-bouts over claret and punch in cracked bowls till morning came, and it was time to follow the hounds. His poor brother was of a much more sober sort, as the lad owned with contrition. So it is that Nature makes folks; and some love books and tea, and some like burgundy and a gallop across country. Our young fellow's tastes were speedily made

visible to his friends in England. None of them were partial to
the Puritan discipline; nor did they like Harry the worse for not
being the least of a milksop. (Chap. 16)

Thackeray undercuts the values of the humble meal and the
American hospitality. As usual he is doing several things at
once, developing his characters and giving us lavish information
about English and American customs of the previous century.
By the time he wrote *The Virginians* he had been to America
twice, in 1852-3 and in 1855-6, on each occasion enjoying hospitality and new friendships, though for many reasons finding
the second tour more exhausting and dispiriting : and he puts into
The Virginians his gratitude and his criticism.[15]
The comic feasts, individually and cumulatively, stand for a
social insight, but play individual parts in the structure, plot
and themes of each novel. The social insight into discord and
false ceremony preceded the novels, and Thackeray's journalism
has many funny and striking pieces on ritual, hospitality and the
quality of cellar[16] and cuisine, most successfully in 'A Little
Dinner at Timmins' (*Punch*, May-July 1848) and the essays on
'Party-Giving Snobs, Dining-Out Snobs and Club Snobs' (*Book
of Snobs*). A comic sociology of feasting, one might say, appears
here without the fiction, but this would be a rather misleading
observation, since Thackeray's journalism, like George Eliot's,
was the beginning of his fiction, and makes lavish use of
novelistic methods in character-sketch and scene-painting. Moreover, this *is* comic sociology, an anatomy of fools and party-
follies. I use the word 'sociology' deliberately, in order to stress
his informativeness about concrete details. If you wanted to
reconstruct the domestic process of giving a dinner in early
Victorian England, you could do no better than go to Thackeray,
because he not only knows and gives the price and suppliers of
everything – food, drink, pots and pans, cutlery, plate, china,
table-linen, service – but provides several estimates, with reasons

[15] He felt strongly that Dickens ought not to have criticized America so
sternly in *American Notes* and *Martin Chuzzlewit* on such a brief acquaintance.
[16] Thackeray's 'Snob' papers are even said to have influenced social
habits, such as the 'dribbling-out' of small quantities of sherry. See Septimus
Berdmore, 'Thackeray', *Westminster Review*, 26 (July 1864), 173. I am
indebted to J. Y. T. Greig (*Thackeray: A Reconsideration*, London, 1950)
for this reference.

for the final choice. Moreover, he gives more than prices and values, throwing in also social psychology – who asks whom and why, and who is not asked, and what the variant responses are to invitation or omission. The device is one of comic exaggeration, typical of *Punch* humour of the period.

What these sketches lack and therefore draw attention to in the treatment of feasts and food in the novels, are not the psychology and the action, but the bad feeling, bitterness and ennui. They are there in a comic form, indicated but not enacted, in the funny melodramatic end of the Timmins. Thackeray observed to a friend that he often intended to be cheerful, but was impelled to gloom and could not resist the dark side. Perhaps nowhere does his pessimism show itself more profoundly and critically than in these feasts, and nowhere do we find a more clear-cut and significant distinction between the record of pleasant experience, the light-hearted journalistic sketch, and the exploration of a corrupt ritual in Vanity Fair, pleasures soured, ceremony disrupted, harmony precarious or false.

CHAPTER SIX

Love

And love illuminates again
The city and the lion's den
W. H. Auden, *New Year Letter*

'You shall love your crooked neighbour
With your crooked heart.'
W. H. Auden, 'As I Walked Out One Evening'

Unlike Dickens, Thackeray does not show a cloistered virtue, in the loving heart of a Dorrit, a Florence Dombey or a Little Nell. Like Dickens, and indeed like most great novelists of the last century and this, he judges human feeling and action by the standard of love, but it is non-transcendent love, a love forced to exist in ordinary everyday circumstances. His world is the world we live in, the world of Vanity Fair, and in it love cannot be free, or pure, or intact; it must be circumscribed and shaped by the society into which it is born and in which it dies or half-dies. Thackeray has no angelic children; indeed his children are very soon conditioned and contaminated by aggressions, greeds and artifices, like eight-year-old Becky Sharp, or Georgy Osborne, or the spoilt Beatrix Castlewood, delighting and persuading her fond parents, or the little girl in *Vanity Fair* – one of his vivid nonce characters – who has a penny and so attracts her companions. He has a few angelic women, Amelia Sedley, Laura and Helen Pendennis, Rachel Castlewood, and the Little Sister of *Philip*, but they are all – with the possible exception of Laura – exposed and tainted. Amelia is one of the characters in *Vanity Fair* who is not a performer and who is capable of love, but the objects of her love are inappropriate, the love itself

F   161

selfish and sometimes unreal, an idolatry attaching itself to fictions, or to parts instead of wholes. Helen loves Pen, and Thackeray shows the possessiveness, unfairness and jealousy of that love, and admits, with an advanced psychological perception, that like other mother-love, it has a sexual element.[1] Rachel loves, and although she is for a long time outwardly unpossessive, loving in secret, her love is exclusive and fiercely jealous. The uncriticized womanly characters, Laura and the Little Sister in *Philip*, are over-idealized in the way of some Dickensian women, but even they are brought firmly into the world. Laura is interestingly streaked with an aggressive feminism[2] – 'the inferior animals have instincts'[3] – and the Little Sister has to fight aggressively and violently. From time to time Thackeray shows his saintly women, especially Helen and Laura, moving out of the world into sanctuaries of prayer and seclusion, but he always brings them again out of the cloister into the Fair. One of his few saintly male characters, Colonel Newcome, becomes more contaminated by the world than any of the women, being as a man necessarily and typically exposed to business, gain and power. His corruptions are the corruptions of loving. He tries to help, to give and to sacrifice for love, but his only means of active loving are those offered by an acquisitive, competitive society. All these people have to act lovingly but with the means that offer, and these means transform the love, taint it, or force it to be possessive and jealous.

In *Vanity Fair* Thackeray compares the unreal, inactive love of Amelia for her dead husband (only a degree more unreal and inactive than her love for him when he was alive) with the generous, active and real love of Dobbin. 'Generous' and 'active' because he gives and helps; 'real' because in loving he does appreciate certain qualities that actually exist : quiet, modesty, sincerity. When Dobbin decides to stop loving because Amelia is a taker and not a giver, there occurs one of those Thackerayan moments of revelation and reversal. It is satisfying as an energetic movement on the part of a too passive character, and also as an act of recognition :

[1] *Pendennis*, Chap. 24.
[2] In *Pendennis* but unfortunately less so in *The Newcomes* and *Philip*, where her reduction to choric status does little for her vitality or individuality.
[3] *The Newcomes*, Chap. 49.

I know what your heart is capable of : it can cling faithfully
to a recollection, and cherish a fancy; but it can't feel such an
attachment as mine deserves to mate with, and such as I would
have won from a woman more generous than you. (Chap. 66)

Amelia, in a natural realization of a lost prize, learns to love, with
a new and real affection, albeit belatedly. Thackeray makes his
celebrated satiric comment on their eventual union, 'Grow green
again, tender little parasite, round the rugged old oak to which
you cling !'

This brings us to an apparent, but deceptive and incomplete
conclusion. Thackeray has introduced this farewell towards the
end of the last chapter, by saying his several farewells to the
characters, and also by saying, 'Here it is – the summit, the end
– the last page of the third volume'. The end of the volume, however, is a metaphor for that last embrace; Thackeray has not yet
reached his last page. When he does, it is to offer an important
qualification of that ending, to make a more tolerant and
charitable gesture of humour that restrospectively revises the
cruel imagery of the green parasite. Like the end of *The Newcomes*, or of *Rowena and Rebecca*, or even of *Esmond*, this is
a kind of happy ending, perhaps the best we can expect in
Vanity Fair.

. . . the Colonel seizing up his little Janey, of whom he is fonder,
than of anything in the world – fonder even than of his 'History
of the Punjaub'.
'Fonder than he is of me,' Emmy thinks, with a sigh. But he
never said a word to Amelia, that was not kind and gentle; or
thought of a want of hers that he did not try to gratify.
(Chap. 67)

Thackeray said in a letter that he intended to show Dobbin
having his desire, and finding the reality rather less than he had
dreamed. The letter is sometimes quoted, however, with a vital
extract missing, the words suggesting that the reality, while
imperfect, offered something, a measure of happiness :

My dear Bell,
Although I have made a rule to myself never to thank critics

yet I like to break it continually, and especially in the present instance for what I hope is the excellent article in Fraser. It seems to me very just in most points as regards the author : some he questions as usual – If I had put in more fresh air as you call it my object would have been defeated – It is to indicate, in cheerful terms, that we are for the most part an abominably foolish and selfish people 'desperately wicked' and all eager after vanities. Everybody is you see in that book – for instance if I had made Amelia a higher order of woman there would have been no vanity in Dobbins falling in love with her, whereas the impression at present is that he is a fool for his pains that he has married a silly little thing and in fact has found out his error rather a sweet and tender one however, *quia multum amavit* I want to leave everybody dissatisfied and unhappy at the end of the story – we ought all to be with our own and all other stories. Good God dont I see (in that may-be cracked and warped looking glass in which I am always looking) my own weaknesses wicked-nesses lusts follies shortcomings? in company let us hope with better qualities about which we will pretermit discourse. We must lift up our voices about these and howl to a congregation of fools : so much at least has been my endeavour. You have all of you taken my misanthropy to task – I wish I could myself : but take the world by a certain standard (you know what I mean) and who dares talk of having any virtue at all? For instance Forster says After a scene with Blifil, the air is cleared by a laugh of Tom Jones – Why Tom Jones in my holding is as big a rogue as Blifil. Before God he is – I mean the man is selfish according to his nature as Blifil according to his. In fact I've a strong im-pression that we are most of us not fit for – never mind.

Pathos I hold should be very occasional indeed in humourous works and indicated rather than expressed or expressed very rarely. In the passage where Amelia is represented as trying to separate herself from the boy – She goes upstairs and leaves him with his aunt 'as that poor Lady Jane Grey tried the axe that was to separate her slender life' I say that is a fine image whoever wrote it (& I came on it quite by surprise in a review the other day) that is greatly pathetic I think : it leaves you to make your own sad pictures – We shouldn't do much more than that I think in comic books – In a story written in the pathetic key it would be different & then the comedy perhaps should be occasional. Some day – but a truce to egotistical twaddle. It seems to me such a time ago that VF was written that one may talk of it as of some body elses performance. (*Letters,* Vol. II, pp. 423-5)

Dobbin and Amelia, in their qualified happy-ever-after, make us feel uncomfortable, but not wholly so : 'rather a sweet and tender one however'. It is typical of Thackeray, of his warmth and melancholy, that he should avoid the black, cynical or pessimistic ending. Dobbin was not an idolatrous lover like Amelia, and what he loved did bear some resemblance to the real woman. Moreover, although Thackeray shows people changing, the changes are never very great ones, as both Kathleen Tillotson[4] and Jean Sudrann[5] have made clear. His purpose in *Vanity Fair*, as in *Pendennis*, was to show people coming to see themselves and other people more clearly, living more truly because more completely, less deludedly or self-deludedly. Thackeray has a remarkable and moving capacity for showing the sadness of love, but also its measured content, moments of peace, approaches to fulfilment. The chequered mortal happiness is an essential part of his social and his psychological picture. It presents some glimpse of the free and natural man, while insisting on the restrictions and corruptions of love.

The most familiar instance of chequered happiness is in the conclusion to *Vanity Fair*, but there are glimpses elsewhere in the novel. Thackeray shows, for instance, that something like happiness may be found in the relaxed, the off-duty, the unlooked-for experience, perhaps more reliably than in the intense climactic joys. The sober and usually brief happiness is no doubt highly expressive of his own experience, with his friends, or with his daughters, or with Jane Brookfield, and it is perhaps for this reason that he is both so concrete and so animated in the records of such measured happiness. It comes from love, but from undemanding moods and modes of love. It is there, very plainly, in the holiday Dobbin and Amelia take in Pumpernickel, and may very well be called a holiday happiness, snatched from the quotidian life, transient, relaxed, undemanding and uncommitted :

Perhaps it was the happiest time of both their lives indeed, if they did but know it – and who does? Which of us can point out and say that was the culmination – that was the summit of

4 *Novels of the Eighteen-Forties.*
5 Jean Sudrann, op. cit.

human joy? But at all events, this couple were very decently contented and enjoyed as pleasant a summer tour as any pair that left England that year. Georgy was always present at the play, but it was the Major who put Emmy's shawl on after the entertainment; and in the walks and excursions the young lad would be on a-head, and up a tower-stair or a tree, whilst the soberer couple were below, the Major smoking his cigar with great placidity and constancy, whilst Emmy sketched the site or the ruin. (Chap. 62)

It is during this episode that Thackeray makes it quite clear that his imperfect hero and his imperfect heroine were really responding to something that existed in each other. We have the splendid comment:

And it must be remembered, that this poor lady had never met a gentleman in her life until this present moment. Perhaps these are rarer personages than some of us think for. Which of us can point out many such in his circle – men whose aims are generous, whose truth is constant, and not only constant in its kind, but elevated in its degree; whose want of meanness makes them simple: who can look the world honestly in the face with an equal manly sympathy for the great and the small? We all know a hundred whose coats are very well made, and a score who have excellent manners, and one or two happy beings who are what they call, in the inner circles, and have shot into the very centre and bull's eye of the fashion; but of gentlemen how many? Let us take a little scrap of paper and each make out his list.
My friend the Major I write, without any doubt, in mine. He had very long legs, a yellow face, and a slight lisp, which at first was rather ridiculous. But his thoughts were just, his brains were fairly good, his life was honest and pure, and his heart warm and humble. He certainly had very large hands and feet, which the two George Osbornes used to caricature and laugh at; and their jeers and laughter perhaps led poor little Emmy astray as to his worth. But have we not all been misled about our heroes, and changed our opinions a hundred times? Emmy, in this happy time, found that hers underwent a very great change in respect of the merits of the Major. (Ibid.)

And this, of Amelia:

You see she has not had too much of that sort of existence as

yet, and has not fallen in the way of means to educate her tastes
or her intelligence. She has been domineered over hitherto by
vulgar intellects. It is the lot of many a woman. And as every
one of the dear sex is the rival of the rest of her kind, timidity
passes for folly in their charitable judgments; and gentleness for
dulness; and silence – which is but timid denial of the unwelcome
assertion of ruling folks, and tacit protestantism – above all, finds
no mercy at the hands of the female Inquisition. (Ibid.)

The minor pleasures and parentheses of love, these he records,
but love as the goal, the climax, the fruition, is very rare in
Thackeray; all except one portrayal of such love are disappoint-
ingly stereotyped and inflated in feeling. Indeed, this is the point
of his parody of happy endings :

> He has got the prize he has been trying for all his life. The bird
> has come in at last. There it is with its head on his shoulder,
> billing and cooing close up to his heart, with soft outstretched
> fluttering wings. This is what he has asked for every day and
> hour for eighteen years. This is what he pined after. Here it is –
> the summit, the end – the last page of the third volume.
> (Chap. 67)

But the chronicling of these holidays of content, far from being
cynical, is a source of refreshment for characters and readers
alike. It is a refreshment even enjoyed, very briefly, by a character
incapable of love, Becky Sharp, whose famous words, 'I think
I could be a good woman if I had five thousand a year', occur
in one of her respites from the whirl and the climb :

> One day followed another, and the ladies of the house passed
> their life in those calm pursuits and amusements which satisfy
> country ladies. Bells rang to meals, and to prayers. The young
> ladies took exercise on the piano-forte every morning after
> breakfast, Rebecca giving them the benefit of her instruction.
> Then they put on thick shoes and walked in the park or
> shrubberies, or beyond the palings into the village, descending
> upon the cottages, with Lady Southdown's medicine, and tracts
> for the sick people there. . . .
> 'It isn't difficult to be a country gentleman's wife,' Rebecca
> thought. 'I think I could be a good woman if I had five thousand
> a year. I could dawdle about in the nursery, and count the

168 *The Exposure of Luxury*

apricots on the wall. I could water plants in a green-house, and pick off dead leaves from the geraniums.' (Chap. 41)

Becky's flight of fancy is not, I think, entirely satirical on Thackeray's part, and it is interesting to see an emotional link between the various chronicles of muted happiness, showing, as they do, Thackeray's refusal to differentiate sharply between the lives of the good and the bad. Becky is the nearest approach to a monster in *Vanity Fair*, but her life is shown with a con- siderable degree of emotional realism. The everyday contented routine is visibly the same experience that is available to Dobbin, Amelia and Lady Jane Crawley.

This acceptance of a moderate happiness marks Thackeray's ending in several stories, from the Christmas story, *Rowena and Rebecca*, to *The Newcomes*. In *Rowena and Rebecca* he is pleasantly indulging himself by rewriting Scott's ending, and bringing it nearer to his heart's desire, like Maggie Tulliver, avenging the dark heroine. But being Thackeray, it is a very muted happy-ever-after :

> Married I am sure they were, and adopted little Cedric; but I don't think they had any other children, or were subsequently very boisterously happy. Of some sort of happiness melancholy is a characteristic, and I think these were a solemn pair, and died rather early. (*Rebecca and Rowena*, Chap. 7)

I suppose it reflects Thackeray's grasp of reality, as well as his mixture of wryness and affection towards his characters, that this should strike us as a very solid happy ending, enfolding the resurrected Ivanhoe and Rebecca with the gentleness of a blessing. The lack of children, the solemnness, and the 'rather early' death act as reassuring realities, qualifications of total bliss which not only keep us in touch with the real world, but create a propitiatory ritual, truly and safely claiming only a little.

Although we tend to think of the evasive ending of *The Newcomes* as a compromise, reached rather uneasily to please the readers as a concession rather like Dickens's revision of the end of *Great Expectations*, it is completely in line with the endings of *Vanity Fair*. It is a kind of happy ending, perhaps

more disturbing than either an unclouded happy ending or an
unhappy one. It stands with the end of *Villette* as a reminder
of the unreality of novels and of the reality of unhappiness or
moderate content outside novels. It also proffers the most uncomfortable reminder of all, that of the reader's preference for
escape and comfort in fiction. James Russell Lowell wrote that
Thackeray knew that Clive and Ethel did not really have a
happy ending :

> I complained of his marrying Clive and Ethel as an artistic
> blunder. He acknowledged that it was so. 'But then, you see,
> what could a fellow do? So many people wanted 'em married.
> To be sure, I had to kill off poor little Rosey rather suddenly,
> but shall not a man do what he will with his own? Besides, we
> can hope they won't have any children.'[6]

Thackeray manages to tease the reader into a realization of the
fiction and, breaking illusion, forces an awareness of the difference between fables and real life. He also manages to shift the
narrative from realistic story to fable, from the narrator, Pendennis, to a more abstract and more realistic 'I'. By so doing
he has the best of both worlds, the happy completion and the
undermining insistence that life would not be like this, that
social pressures scarcely permit such magical release and freedom
for love. At the same time, he achieves another form of abstract
pathos that we sometimes find in self-conscious novelists, a
nostalgic appeal for the fictional character, in which the sadness
of his fictitiousness and the realization that the real-life equivalent
would be even sadder, are curiously and poignantly interwoven;
it is also an effect, and indeed, almost a cadence, which
Thackeray very plainly learnt from Charles Lamb, whose essay
'Dream-children' is echoed and toughened at the end of *The
Newcomes* :

> As I write the last line with a rather sad heart, Pendennis and
> Laura, and Ethel and Clive, fade away into fable-land. I hardly
> know whether they are not true; whether they do not live near
> us somewhere. They were alive, and I heard their voices; but

[6] *Letters of James Russell Lowell*, ed. Charles Eliot Norton, 2 vols (New
York, 1894), Vol. 1, pp. 238-9. Ray quotes this in *Letters*, Vol. III,
p. 465 n.

five minutes since was touched by their grief. And have we
parted with them here on a sudden, and without so much as a
shake of the hand? Is yonder line (——) which I drew with my
own pen, a barrier between me and Hades as it were, across which
I can see those figures retreating and only dimly glimmering?
Before taking leave of Mr Arthur Pendennis, might he not have
told whether Miss Ethel married anyone finally? It was provoking
that he should retire to the shades without answering that
sentimental question. (Chap. 80)

Arthur has to retire to the shades as well as the other characters, because he would have known the answer, so Thackeray
comes on as the real author, in Switzerland with his children.[7]
His status is comically very blurred indeed. In the little wood
where he 'strayed' for a while, the story of the novel was
'revealed' somehow – it is very like *Alice in Wonderland*. And
at the end, which he is not supposed to know, he takes us back
and suggests, by the use of deduction, that this and this might
or must have happened, and concludes with speculation:

> My belief then is, that in fable-land somewhere, Ethel and Clive
> are living most comfortably together : that she is immensely fond
> of his little boy, and a great deal happier now than they would
> have been had they married at first. . . .
> But have they any children? I, for my part, should like her
> best without, and entirely devoted to little Tommy. But for you,
> dear friend, it is as you like. You may settle your fable-land in
> your own fashion. Anything you like happens in fable-land.
> (Ibid.)

The self-consciousness, playfulness and evasiveness (three separate
aspects of the teasing at the end) work together to relate the
happy ending to the individual and common fantasy-life, and
to our own fable-land. By this means he refuses to end in the
realistic mode.

While Thackeray's sentiment and satire, lovingness and
melancholy, come together in *The Newcomes* to show love, they

[7] Thackeray was indeed in Switzerland, and in Berne with his children,
two years before he finished *The Newcomes*, in the summer of 1853, as he
describes at the beginning of its conclusion. During his month in Switzerland
he wrote Numbers 2 and 3 (Chaps 4-9) of the novel.

do not show it winning any great prizes. The realistic ending –
our last view of the characters – leaves us with Ethel and Clive
subdued by life, Ethel ennobled, but Clive soured. Into Clive, as
more or less consistently into all his heroes, Thackeray puts his
own melancholy, his *atra cura*, as he very often called it.
Warrington's love is bitter, because he has made a fool of himself
and can't have Laura – making her in love with Warrington was
a fine stroke, providing, perhaps, the only strength in her very
weak character. Clive is bitter because he is even worse off than
Warrington, who at least is not required by society to live with
his *mésalliance*. For a while, even Pendennis is bitter. Although
the presentation of love in Pendennis is unstable, and often
sentimental, at times Thackeray hits on a novel device for
showing genuine love, by undermining it. He finds a comic
medium for it, insisting that love is a fresh, genuine, exciting,
unrepeatable experience, yet he is rueful and wry about it.
When the character is not a melancholy lover, the novelist is.

At the beginning of *Pendennis*, where we find Pen in love,
he is certainly not melancholy but, on the contrary, not looking
before or after, and accordingly greatly pleased with life. Thackeray manages very well to show Pen as a quixotic lover, mis-
taking the Dulcinea for an ideal, and he does this not only by
using Cervantic situations, like the dinner where we see through
Pen's eyes and through a more realistic pair of our own, but
through a brilliant use of comic and yet respectful imagery. The
two chief images, one of the horse (so quixotic) and one of the
sea, are both used indulgently and wittily and these are excellent
instances of Thackeray's charitable satire and a detached
presentation of the passions. We see Pen's passionate desires
with amusement, but with affection, not coldness. (It is amusing,
incidentally, to see Thackeray making a comic use of the symbol
of the horse, to be used so much more seriously for passion by
George Eliot, and so much more passionately by D. H. Lawrence.) Here is Pen as Quixote :

Pen had even less sleep that night than on the night before.
In the morning, and almost before dawn, he went out and saddled
that unfortunate Rebecca himself, and rode her on the Downs
like mad. Again Love had roused him – and said, 'Awake,
Pendennis, I am here.' That charming fever – that delicious

longing – and fire, and uncertainty; he hugged them to him – he
would not have lost them for all the world. (Chap. 5)

And again, a little earlier, Pen's passionate riding crosses with
Smirke's, in a firm statement of a serious and comic love-plot.
Neither Pen nor Smirke is treated realistically though both are
genuine, and in the end it is Smirke's example, criticized by
Pen, which acts as a rebuke and a shameful mirror :

> He went gently at first, but galloped like a madman as soon as he
> thought that he was out of hearing.
> Smirke, thinking of his own affairs, and softly riding with his
> toes out, to give Pen his three hours' reading at Fairoaks, met
> his pupil, who shot by him like the wind. Smirke's pony shied,
> as the other thundered past him; the gentle curate went over
> his head among the stinging-nettles in the hedge. Pen laughed as
> they met, pointed towards the Baymouth road, and was gone
> half a mile in that direction before poor Smirke had picked
> himself up.
> Pen had resolved in his mind that he *must* see Foker that
> morning; he must hear about her; know about her; be with
> somebody who knew her; and honest Smirke, for his part, sitting
> up among the stinging-nettles, as his pony cropped quietly in the
> hedge, thought dismally to himself, ought he to go to Fairoaks
> now that his pupil was evidently gone away for the day? Yes,
> he thought he might go, too. He might go and ask Mrs Pen-
> dennis when Arthur would be back; and hear Miss Laura her
> Watts's Catechism. He got up on the little pony – both were used
> to his slipping off – and advanced upon the house from which
> his scholar had just rushed away in a whirlwind.
> Thus love makes fools of all of us, big and little; and the
> curate had tumbled over head and heels in pursuit of it, and
> Pen had started in the first heat of the mad race. (Chap. 4)

Thackeray manages to modulate from satire to sympathy, and
so avoid mere ridicule, by the engaging generalization which
insists on the common experience and disclaims a superior
attitude : 'Thus love makes fools of all of us' and 'He did not
yet know what was coming' and 'Was Titania the first who fell
in love with an ass, or Pygmalion the only artist who has gone
crazy about a stone? . . . He flung himself into the stream and
drank with all his might. Let those who have been thirsty own

how delicious that first draught is.' He also makes the experience physically vivid,[8] which gives the passion substance, and calls for sympathy. Pen is always shown in violent motion, either literally, on his horse, or metaphorically, drinking and flinging. The passion's recklessness, its longing, its heat, are all shown, as in *Romeo and Juliet*, though more comically. The natural need and the rush are also shown, sadly and comically, as being quite independent of appropriate objects.

One more image illustrates this comic sympathy for Pen's first love; it is in exaggerated and yet accurate language because the passion itself is marked by excess:

> Then Pen went down the rock, and walked about on the sand, biting his nails by the shore of the much-sounding sea. It stretched before him bright and immeasurable. The blue waters came rolling into the bay, foaming and roaring hoarsely: Pen looked them in the face with blank eyes, hardly regarding them. What a tide there was pouring into the lad's own mind at the time, and what a little power had he to check it! Pen flung stones into the sea, but it still kept coming on. (Chap. 5)

Again there is the physical energy; the sense of age looking at youth in 'the lad'; something comic, the mock-heroic of the grand description, 'the much-sounding sea' 'bright and immeasurable'; and yet its imaged brilliance, exhilaration, power. Thackeray's yokings preserve the passion while observing its excess, 'biting his nails by the shore of the much-sounding sea', Pen 'flung stones into the sea, but it still kept coming on'. This kind of rise and fall he could have learnt from Fielding, though it is Thackeray's own achievement to make such conjunctions and such movement in so small a space. Thackeray's sentences achieve here what Fielding's modulations in paragraphs often do. But, of course, the attempt is different. Thackeray is trying to say, all the time, that this is amusing to contemplate, but absolutely real; that it is funny from the outside but agony inside; that its very violence and extremity make it material for satire and for sympathy; that it is comical and awful; that Pen is a fool but in the grip of something serious; that he is small

[8] In many respects it is like Dickens's account of David Copperfield's several experiences of calf-love, but although they are comic and sympathetic, they are not shown as physically urgent and strong, as in Thackeray.

and it is big, and so on. And always implying, one way or another, that there is a certain familiar experience here, and something to be valued, as real, as strong.

Thackeray is able to infuse a sympathetic dramatization of strong feeling with his own melancholy, without too great a withdrawal from the scene. When George Eliot, for instance, wishes to make a wry comment on innocence, from the standpoint of experience, she juxtaposes her melancholy wisdom with the pure feelings of the characters. Thackeray chooses a more ironic and complex method, unifying the two points of view, infusing the inevitable sadness of experience into the wholeheartedness of youth. It is a special form of his comedy, typically drawing the two feelings together, qualifying but not destroying by melancholy. It is a blending device which seems to come naturally from an experience where happiness is seen so moderately, and where melancholy is not sour, but warmed and lit with affection and gratitude. In his presentation of Clive and Ethel, Thackeray is trying to catch something rather difficult. There are stages when Ethel can hold Clive off by flirtation and mere cousinly affection, just as there are later stages, after he is married, when she can be unaffectedly affectionate. But there is an awkward and interesting middle stage when Ethel and Pen enjoy the intimate privacy of meetings in Madame de Florac's old garden in Paris, though no actual commitments have been made, nor indeed will be made, except between the lines. Thackeray in fact makes sure that we shall be able to read between the lines by putting nothing else between them; he withdraws his own authorial commentary and uses dramatic dialogue, as he does elsewhere in *The Newcomes*. The scene is marked by gravity and reticence, especially in the last dialogue, after Madame de Florac has told them that they cannot go on meeting in her house. The scene ends with a vibrant sadness and sympathy, permitted by Thackeray's sentimental use of literal translation from the French, as in 'she loves thee? I know she loves thee', but the dialogue at its best is more restrained.

ETHEL : And do you think you will never be able to paint as well as M. Delaroche?
CLIVE : No – never.
ETHEL : And – and – you will never give up painting?

CLIVE : No – never. That would be like leaving your friend who was poor; or deserting your mistress, because you were disappointed about her money.

However, Thackeray gets his best effect of comic melancholy from an archetypal garden scene, which has a slightly comic romanticism.

. . . [T]wo young people are walking up and down in an avenue of lime-trees, which are still permitted to grow in that ancient place. In the centre of that avenue is a fountain, surmounted by a Triton so grey and moss-eaten, that though he holds his conch to his swelling lips, curling his tail in the arid basin, his instrument has had a sinecure for at least fifty years; and did not think fit even to play when the Bourbons, in whose time he was erected, came back from their exile. At the end of the lime-tree avenue is a broken-nosed damp Faun, with a marble panpipe, who pipes to the spirit ditties which I believe never had any tune. . . . There is Cupid, who has been at the point of kissing Psyche this half-century at least, though the delicious event has never come off, through all those blazing summers and dreary winters : there is Venus and her Boy under the damp little dome of a cracked old temple. (Chap. 47)

Thackeray's mythological and literary allusions are frequently comic, not only in order to depreciate pretence or shallowness, but to achieve this kind of bitter-sweet feeling. In this passage he combines the Keatsian longing and ecstasy with classical sensuality and pain; this synthesis permits him to take a wry look at these modern lovers and modern love, and to sigh and pity, and place in perspective. The most obvious effect is the placing in time,[9] but I suggest it is also important to see the comic and battered imagery of love used here for Ethel's worldliness and faint, if genuine, feeling. This is a dismal love-story, and the dampness and cracks and broken-down statuary belong to melancholy.

I am not suggesting that Thackeray's melancholy is a way of avoiding sentimentality. Like Charles Lamb, he uses the comic in order to create a defence within the pathetic mode, and his

[9] See Jean Sudrann, op. cit., 380-3.

AT THE HÔTEL DE FLORAC

jokes and ironies are often permissive. A strong instance of this comic licence for sentimental melancholy occurs in another rather desolate and half-articulated love-scene, between Pen and Laura, again at a stage when one of the lovers is partly engaged, partly disengaged, but confusedly enjoying and lamenting the situation, and half-dramatizing cynicism. This aspect of Pen also shows him playing, in a different relationship, as he played with Blanche. He has given Laura a bit of honey-suckle, seen his mother's grave, and is taken first with the thought of dead vain desires, and then with the subsequent thought, 'what does it matter for the little space?' :

> 'But will come in spite of us. But is reflection. But is the sceptic's familiar, with whom he has made a compact; and if he forgets it, and indulges in happy day-dreams, or building of air-castles, or listens to sweet music, let us say, or to the bells ringing to church, But taps at the door, and says, "Master, I am here. You are my master; but I am yours. Go where you will you can't travel without me. I will whisper to you when you are on your knees at church. I will be at your marriage pillow. I will sit down at your table with your children. I will be behind your death-bed curtain."' (Chap. 71)

This fine melodramatic set-speech shows the cynic's temptation. It is also Pen's oblique way of making love to Laura, to whom he cannot honourably declare his feelings. But as soon as Pen is free for the union with Laura, the melancholy is shed, even though he continues to be spoken of as a writer of realistic and cynical novels. The melancholy is in part used to describe love qualified and restricted, its joys 'finely chequered' and '*à la mortal*', as Jane Austen calls it. It is also used indulgently and sentimentally on occasion, as in the 'But' speech, which is one of the rare examples of Thackeray's 'fine writing', a thing that he abhorred.

Thackeray is not wholly in control of Pendennis's melancholy. It is sometimes placed and criticized as indulgent, or, at least, histrionic, but there are many occasions where it is presented without demur, as in the conversations between Warrington and Laura. Thackeray sometimes manages to get at a distance from Pendennis, sometimes not, and the difficulty may be that experienced by Dickens with David Copperfield or by George

Eliot with Maggie Tulliver, in handling a character with marked
autobiographical features, who is sufficiently objectified to be
criticized, but not quite steadily or completely. In one novel,
however, Thackeray managed to create his melancholy character
in a perfectly unified and dynamic form. That novel was *Henry
Esmond*.

At first sight, it seems strange that Esmond should be Thackeray's most controlled and analysed melancholy lover, since he
appears in the one novel which is not a large-scale satiric venture,
and in which the disengaging arts of comedy are extremely
muted. However, the exceptional psychological clarity of Esmond
as a character is on reflection less odd. It is a psychological
novel, and the passions are both centrally and analytically
presented. The analysis goes underground, however, in the
portrayal of Rachel Castlewood's hidden love for Esmond which
is presented in scenes of ambiguous emotion. Her maternal
anxiety and fury when Harry brings smallpox from the village
inn, for instance, turns out to be jealousy about his flirtation with
Nancy Sievebright, and her betrayal of grief about Harry's
accident makes her husband jealous of Lord Mohun, not Henry
Esmond. Analysis also moves underground in the major
emotional action of Henry Esmond's love for Beatrix Castlewood
and her mother Rachel. Much has already been written about
the love-story of *Esmond*,[10] especially its subtleties of dramatic
presentation and its possible psychological roots in Thackeray's
experience; I will therefore confine myself to one or two aspects
of his analysis of love.

The celebrated end of *Esmond*, in which we move violently
and abruptly from the death of Esmond's love for Beatrix to
his happy marriage with Rachel, is functionally and most
eloquently abrupt, and neither clumsy nor evasive. In a way,
it is unlike Thackeray's commonly muted happy endings and
his refusal to show love as a climactic or conclusive prize. But as
in *Vanity Fair*, there is a double ending: we have the end of a
fictional construction made by the characters, which is followed
by the ending of the whole story, the reader's fiction. In *Vanity*

---

[10] See, for example: J. Y. T. Greig, *Thackeray: A Reconsideration*;
Geoffrey Tillotson, *Thackeray the Novelist*; John Loofbourow, *Thackeray
and the Form of Fiction*; John E. Tilford, Jr, 'The Love-Theme of *Henry
Esmond*', *PMLA*, 67 (1952), 684-701, and ' "Unsavoury Plot" of *Henry
Esmond*', *NCF*, 6 (September 1951), 121-30.

Fair Thackeray showed the end of Dobbin's desire, and in the margin beyond showed how living has to survive certain endings. In *Esmond*, he images the end of Esmond's life-fiction, and in the margin beyond shows how survival may sometimes bring new gains after all. The melancholy loss of Esmond's fiction about Beatrix, about his striking heroic and revolutionary role, about the Pretender, and about England, is succeeded by another story, and one, it is implied, which is less like a 'drama' : 'With the sound of King George's trumpets, all the vain hopes of the weak and foolish young Pretender were blown away; and with that music, too, I may say, the drama of my own life was ended.' (*Esmond*, Bk 3, Chap. 13)

If the images for his passions and illusions were 'music' and 'drama', the new image for the happy-ever-after with Rachel is that of the American Indian summer, and its emphasis is quiet. There are two kinds of quiet here, that of the relationship itself, for which words like 'calmest', 'serene' and 'rest' are used, and that of the narrator's reticence :

> That happiness, which hath subsequently crowned it, cannot be written in words; 'tis of its nature sacred and secret, and not to be spoken of, though the heart be ever so full of thankfulness, save to Heaven and the One Ear alone – to one fond being, the truest and tenderest and purest wife ever man was blessed with.
>
> (Bk 3, Chap. 13)

The joining of 'secret' to 'sacred' makes the conclusion erotic as well as ideal, and its emotional particularization reminds me of Coventry Patmore's erotic joining of sacred and profane love, on which Gerard Manley Hopkins commented, 'That's telling secrets'. The ending is a kind of evasion, no doubt, but it seems to be also a deliberately quiet way of describing happiness. In *Vanity Fair*, *Rowena and Rebecca* and *The Newcomes*, Thackeray declines to commit himself to more than a speculative and provisional fantasy of sober content. In *Esmond*, he does want to make high claims, and in the running title makes Esmond call his love 'My crowning happiness'. Esmond claims, 'Sure, love *vincit omnia*; is immeasurably above all ambition, more precious than wealth, more noble than name', and says 'he hath not felt the highest faculty of the soul who hath not enjoyed it'. The reticence suggests privacy and reverence.

In accord with this restraint, and perhaps accounting for it, is the surprising nature of the last 'crowning happiness', which does come unexpectedly upon Esmond, as a second attachment of a different and better kind. The word 'crowning' is not merely a traditional metaphor. In one sentence, quoted above, Thackeray speaks of the sound of King George's trumpets blowing away the vain hopes of the Pretender, and takes up the 'music' which ends the Pretender's hopes, to end also his hopes and 'drama'. In the same way the image of the lost crown surely recurs in the next sentence : ' . . . and with that music, too, I may say, the drama of my own life was ended. That happiness, which hath subsequently crowned it. . . .' Both the image of the crown and the image of the conquest (*amor vincit omnia*) are revived and refreshed images in this novel, which is not only about real crowns and conquests, but about the contamination of love by crowns and conquests. When Esmond speaks of the highest faculty of the soul employed in love, when he esteems it above ambition, more precious than wealth, more noble than name, he is not indulging in hyperbole for conclusion and triumph, but consummating the moral action of the novel.

Thackeray joins most subtly many aspects of loving; its obsessions, its pangs, its snatched strong moments, its transports, its moderate contents and its possessiveness. He is a marvellous chronicler of jealousy, and his portrait of Rachel, for instance, is a brilliant and versatile rendering of repression and releases, sometimes rendered in silence, sometimes overcome in noble self-effacing generosity, sometimes insistently betrayed in the tapping of a foot, sometimes bursting out in hostility. Like her jealousy, too, is her passion for Esmond. It is a rational passion, like Dobbin's and Amelia's, in desiring an appropriate object after an inappropriate one, but it often shows itself irrationally, in anger, coldness and hostility. Thackeray's rendering of the *odi* in the *amo* is the more complex for being done implicitly and dramatically. It is sometimes shown without explanation, sometimes accompanied by ambiguous explanations, sometimes then slowly revealed and brought into a light which illuminates past darknesses. The loves of Rachel, Beatrix and Esmond are more than studies in passion and jealousy; they are very carefully placed analyses of love in the environment of emulation, ambition, and acquisition. The explicit and radical theme of *Henry Esmond* is implicit but more subdued and subordinated than the social satire in the other novels. It is the theme of the corruptions of love in the corrupt society. Love exists, and is better than 'name', 'wealth' and 'ambition', but it cannot transcend them entirely. Working back from the end, then, we find a love which is not 'above all ambition', not 'more precious than wealth', and not 'more noble than name'. Esmond's ambitions were created by his attempts to win and buy love, through going to war, winning money and name, and making complicated sacrifice of legitimacy and name for love's sake.

The novel begins with Thackeray's insistence on its dehistoricizing aims : 'Why shall History go on kneeling to the end of time? I am for having her rise up off her knees, and take a natural posture. . . . In a word, I would have History familiar rather than heroic. . . .' (Bk 1, Introduction) His way of making history familiar is twofold. He shows historical events and characters in ordinary quotidian life, in so far as this is possible (with military events, for instance, it is less easy than with literature or politics), and he shows the private and personal motivation of historical events. In this respect, he is at first sight doing something bizarre in the history of the Victorian novel, which is on the whole engaged in the rather more modern enterprise of historicizing private events, showing the social and economic basis or background to the personal life, the public shaping of the individual story. But we have already seen that in *Vanity Fair*, *Pendennis* and *The Newcomes* Thackeray is also doing what Dickens and George Eliot do in *Great Expectations* and *Middlemarch*, in attempting to show the public pressures that shape our personal dramas. But although *Esmond* does dehistoricize the public life, showing the pursuit of war, fame, literary glory and honour as enterprises undertaken for love, there is also, as in the social novels, the analysis of a determining public life. All the persons of the novel are shown as directed by acquisitiveness, ambition, reputation and emulation. Esmond is not set apart from the others; he is initially shown as loving[11]

[11] It is interesting to note that his need for love is like that of two other noble bastards in Victorian novels, Esther Summerson, who is really illegitimate, and Daniel Deronda, who, like Esmond, believes that he is illegitimate.

and generous, and then as being contaminated by social ends. Afterwards he finds that the pursuit of title, crown, glory, honour and love end in a betrayal and disillusion : the Pretender cares more for a beautiful woman than for a crown, Beatrix cares more for money and rank than for love or politics, the Duke of Marlborough cares more for fame than honour. His own pursuits of the ideal are also vanities and he returns to the nearest thing to a free and unconditioned love, the devoted, suffering, unworldly constancy of Rachel.

That is only a crude outline of the novel's causality. Thackeray's full achievement is to dramatize the individual psychology of these intricate social and moral relations. In so doing, he shows a man in love with two women, something many of his contemporary readers found startling and even disgusting. (In this connection, it is interesting to see Thackeray himself, though perhaps not very seriously, criticizing Charlotte Brontë in *Villette* for showing a 'good woman' ready to love two men, and objecting that if he had done that Miss Brontë would have been the first to object – a fine example of the double standard in literary criticism.) From the beginning of *Esmond*, we see Esmond's obsessed and plainly sexual passion for Beatrix, which may well ironically show the pursuit of an ideal Beatrice. We also see his more muted, passive, grateful devotion to 'his mistress', Rachel Castlewood, eight years his elder. Thackeray blurs and prepares for the end by ambiguity of words such as 'love', 'devotion' 'dear', 'dearest', 'heart' and 'mistress'. ('Mistress' is a special case of ambiguity, carrying with it the connotation of actual service, remote adoration and amorous relationship.) The vagueness of emotional terminology stands Thackeray in good stead. But the early stages are also presented in ways which relate to Thackeray's feeling for Jane Brookfield, especially to his sense that she was a suffering and patient wife of an unworthy husband, a view coming more naturally than reliably from the unsatisfied lover. Thackeray also presents the ease and comfort of the moderate happiness, with no transports, but the undemanding pleasures of company and affinity :

> But if the children were careless, 'twas a wonder how eagerly the mother learned from her young tutor – and taught him too. The happiest instinctive faculty was this lady's – a faculty for discerning latent beauties and hidden graces of books, especially

books of poetry, as in a walk she would spy out field-flowers and
make posies of them, such as no other hand could. She was a
critic not by reason but by feeling; the sweetest commentator
of those books they read together; and the happiest hours of
young Esmond's life, perhaps, were those past in the company
of this kind mistress and her children. (Bk 1, Chap. 9)

Throughout the novel Thackeray shows Rachel's reticence, guilt
and jealousy; and also Esmond's devotion, gratitude and contented companionship.

The interweaving of the two loves is presented from the very
beginning, in the Preface to the 'memoirs' purporting to be
written by the 'editor', his daughter Rachel. She is made to
emphasize three aspects of feeling: the passionate and exclusive
devotion of 'her mother' (unnamed) for Esmond; his affection
for his wife, suggested with effective vagueness; and his feeling
that Beatrix was peerless, flashing out in her defence, even though
dishonoured. The sentence is loaded with the weight of an old
attachment, fidelity to the past. The weight is heavily impressed
on us in a reply to a jealous comment:

. . . After visiting her, my poor mamma said she had lost all her
good looks, and warned me not to set too much store by any
such gifts which nature had bestowed upon me. She grew exceedingly stout; and I remember my brother's wife, Lady
Castlewood, saying 'No wonder she became a favourite, for the
King likes them old and ugly, as his father did before him.' On
which papa said – 'All women were alike; that there was never
one so beautiful as that one; and that we could forgive her
everything but her beauty.' And hereupon my mamma looked
vexed. . . . (Preface)

The retrospects of Henry Esmond, like those of David Copperfield, form the medium of the narrative, shifting from foreground
to background, past to present. From time to time we are
reminded of the retrospect by the shifts from third person to
first, from 'Henry Esmond' to 'Colonel Esmond' to 'the writer
of this memoir' to 'I'.[12] The 'I' is often used eloquently to mark

[12] Names and name are particularly important in a novel about legitimacy
and reputation. Even *The Spectator* paper is thematically important, in this
respect, dealing as it does with a lady who forgets a man's name.

moments of great depth of feeling, though it is by no means used for all those moments. The memorial reconstructions of *Esmond* differ from those of *David Copperfield* or *Jane Eyre* in having a much more pointed psychological purpose. Charlotte Brontë makes Jane revise her innocence in the light of her experience, softening criticism, summing up effort, marking the permanent damage, and so forth. Dickens makes David look with a special comic and pathetic nostalgia at innocence, seeing the sharp irony of a future-haunted past in retrospect, or of the strangeness and silliness of what at the time seemed profound or rational. Both novelists use memory constantly, but have surprisingly little to say about its nature. It is memory's content, not its form, that engages them as they remember and observe how different the past looks as we look back at it, through time, over time, in time. For Thackeray, the experience of remembering is much more analysed and analytic, much closer to Wordsworth's imaginative time-travelling in *The Prelude* through those 'spots of time' which are saturated with the values of deeply felt experience, and so saturated that memory revives and does not weaken them. Thackeray's sense of emotional memory is not involuntary as it is in Proust, and at times in George Eliot, nor is it part of a moral series of related visions, as in Wordsworth. It is perhaps closest of all to Thomas Hardy, for whom also memory is a means of loving, and at times, apparently, a means more reliable than others. *Esmond* is like some of Hardy's best love-lyrics, such as 'Joys of Memory', 'Before Knowledge' or 'During Wind and Rain', in its appreciation and revival of the past passion in a present passion. Thackeray and Hardy both seem most lucid, steady and passionate when the loving is a looking back, a harking back, itself a retrospect, a loving memory. *Esmond* is actually a memorial act of love, secretly addressed to Jane Brookfield in lingering retrospect after the experience is finished, an affectionate fantasy of unacted possibilities. His insistence on love-in-memory may also derive point from the sharp contrast between past and present in the two strongest emotional ties that we know about, the tie to the memory of his young wife, after they were separated by her schizophrenia, as well as the tie to Jane Brookfield, after they 'separated'. But strong as the autobiographical roots must be, the retrospects are also consistent with the presentation of moderate content at the end of *Vanity Fair*, *Rowena and Rebecca* and *The Newcomes*, providing yet another way of showing the limits of love honestly and toughly, without cynicism or devaluation.

Esmond's story is about idolatry and vanity, about his love for one of the most attractive and most corrupt of Thackeray's heroines. Beatrix is corrupt : ambitious for money and rank, often *ennuyée*, self-disgusted, perhaps self-destructive, having a short-lived period of active virtue. In Rachel's Preface we have the first brief but strong flash of Esmond's passion (in the part already quoted) when he says 'there was never one so beautiful'. The retrospect is not an idealized selection by any means, its chronicles including recollections of thwarted desires, painful obsession, 'nights of rage . . . days of torment . . . passionate unfulfilled desire . . . sickening jealousy. . . .' (Bk 2, Chap. 10, 'An Old Story about a Fool and a Woman') Nevertheless, the key sentences draw our attention to the passionate act of memory, making it clear that the novel is about a man who may have found a faithful love, that '*amor vincit omnia*', but also that the man discovers in the act of writing his complex fidelity to the past. Beatrix is a much-criticized character, and so is Esmond as Don Quixote and 'The Faithful Fool'.[13] But the memoir writer, knowing very well that in writing we discover thoughts we did not know we had, writes, remembers, and is restored to the past, which is not destroyed by the satirist or the comedian.[14] It is the opposite of the memorial action in *Jane Eyre* and *David Copperfield*, for Thackeray shows his character penetrating the past experience with a reanimated passion. He does more, he insists that we are everything which we have been; it is not remarkable that our dead loves can rise up easily, never having died :

> How well all things were remembered ! The ancient towers and gables of the Hall darkling against the east, the purple shadows on the green slopes, the quaint devices and carvings of the dial . . . all these were before us, along with a thousand memories of our youth, beautiful and sad, but as real and vivid in our minds as that fair and always-remembered scene our eyes behold

---

[13] Esmond's unacted comedy.
[14] Unlike the early loves of David Copperfield, deflated and drained of genuine feeling by the comic memory.

once more. We forget nothing. The memory sleeps, but wakens
again. . . . (Bk 3, Chap. 7)

and again :

Years after this passion hath been dead and buried, along with
a thousand other worldly cares and ambitions, he who felt it can
recall it out of its grave, and admire, almost as fondly as he did
in his youth, that lovely queenly creature. I invoke that beautiful
spirit from the shades and love her still; or rather I should say
that such a past is always present to a man; such a passion once
felt forms a part of his whole being, and cannot be separated from
it. . . . (Bk 3, Chap. 6)

He compares the imprint of passion to the influence of faith,
poetry, religion, becoming a part of us even if we get over it.
His image for what has marked us, healed, and still remained,
is the scar he got at Blenheim.[15] It is this constant insistence on
the revival of passion that makes *Esmond* more than an act
of memory. Like no other Victorian novel it is an act of invocation. We have to wait for Proust to get such another, though
La recherche du temps perdu is more the finding of an aesthetic
unity in life and art, than a celebration of love. *Esmond* is an
invocation and an act of love.

The beginning and the end of the novel make heroic claims;
one for the virtuous and distinguished Esmond, the other for the
great and noble love of Rachel and Esmond. But in the centre,
there is the story of a limited, unheroic and quotidian love. In
being unheroic, it is very like the unheroic stories of the 'two
great men of the age', as Esmond calls them, Marlborough and
Swift, corrupted, as Thackeray's rudely familiar History Muse
insists, by ambition, ruthlessness, dishonesty and emulation.
Esmond is like them, pursuing his vanity of love (as he admits to
Lord Bolingbroke when they debate their preferences in vanity)
with the other vanities of the age, military, literary and political.
He tries to be a soldier, a wit and a Jacobite revolutionary, in
order to do the most corrupt thing of all, to trade with love,

---

[15] It is worth noticing that he also uses the image of the scar for the
same emphasis when remembering his misery in prison, estranged from
Rachel.

barter for it, and buy it. The love is determined by its conditions, becomes two-faced or two-hearted, corrupt, private. The memoir itself is a most intimate record, happily and ironically misunderstood by its editor, who knows enough about her mother's passion for her father to call it 'so passionate and exclusive as to prevent her, I think, from loving any other person except with an inferior regard; her whole thoughts being centred on this one object of affection and worship'. The novel makes plain that this was not the case with Esmond. Esmond tell us that when he found Beatrix's intrigue with the Pretender his love fell down dead on the spot :

> But her keen words gave no wound to Mr Esmond; his heart was too hard. As he looked at her, he wondered that he could ever have loved her. His love of ten years was over; it fell down dead on the spot, at the Kensington Tavern, where Frank brought him the note out of Eikon Basilike. The Prince blushed and bowed low, as she gazed at him, and quitted the chamber. I have never seen her from that day. (Bk 3, Chap. 13)

The whole novel makes it plain that this is not so, that loves do not die, that the past is still alive.

What the novel achieves as fiction looks confused but is, I suggest, a consistent if complicated proof of what Thackeray so shrewdly sees as the discovery of experience in art : he speaks of finding our thoughts in writing them, and in the novel he finds passions too. He discovers something of their nature and their conditions; war, politics, religion, love, so the parallelisms of event, character and image argue, are similarly determined, and influence and pervert each other. Thackeray involves his hero in all the vanities of competition, acquisition and emulation, and all for love. That love was pain more than pleasure, resulting in what the ironic, but not wholly ironic, narrator calls a 'Diary of drivel', and of 'agonies'. In retrospect, the experience is crowned with the special glory of affectionate memory, still loved on this side – the right side – of idolatry.[16] With irony, rapturous outburst, calm imagery, Thackeray writes his love-story. Its happinesses are either hidden, veiled like the sacred secret love for Rachel, or shown as most stable and joyful when

[16] In *Vanity Fair* Thackeray brings out the unreality of loving the past; in *Esmond* he acknowledges the sense of reality in such an act of memory.

revived in the appreciative acts of memory. The love suggests –
though only in fits and starts – the possibility of triumph over
Vanity Fair. It offers freedom and the conquest of time, but
is still fleshed by vanity, its converse and action shaped by
conquest, competition, honour, rank, money. The carefully
eighteenth-century title, *The History of Henry Esmond, Esq.,
a Colonel in the Service of Her Majesty Queen Anne,* looks up
first sight like a modest withdrawal from Vanity Fair, setting up
the noble Esmond with a mere 'Esq.' and the name of Colonel.
But the novel shows his sacrifice of title, rank and name as one
of the subtlest perversions of honour and love. *Esmond* makes
just as radical an act of social criticism as the other novels, but
it does so from the inside, showing more passionately, and
analytically, the difficulty of love in the great world. It is a great
psychological and a great social novel, the greatness consisting
in the unity of the public and the private worlds.

SELECTED LIST OF NOVELS, STORIES AND LECTURES BY W. M. THACKERAY

1837–8   'The Yellowplush Correspondence' in *Fraser's* (published as *The Yellowplush Papers*, 1852)

1839–40   *Catherine*

1840   *The Paris Sketch-Book*
A Shabby Genteel Story

1844   *The Luck of Barry Lyndon: A Romance of the Last Century*

1846–7   'The Snobs of England, by One of Themselves' in *Punch* (published with revisions in book form as *The Book of Snobs*, 1848)

1847   '*Punch*'s Prize Novelists' (published in book form as *Novels by Eminent Hands*, 1856)

1847–8   *Vanity Fair: Pen and Pencil Sketches of English Society* (title in serial publication, 1847–8); afterwards *Vanity Fair: A Novel without a Hero* (title when published in book form, 1848)

1848–50   *The History of Pendennis: His Fortunes and Misfortunes, His Friends and His Greatest Enemy*

1850   *Rebecca and Rowena: A Romance upon Romance* (first published as 'Proposals for a Continuation of "Ivanhoe" ' in *Fraser's*, 1846)

1852   *The History of Henry Esmond, Esq., a Colonel in the Service of Her Majesty Q. Anne, Written by Himself*

1853   *The English Humourists of the Eighteenth Century: A Series of Lectures Delivered in England, Scotland and the United States of America* (delivered 1851)

1853–5   *The Newcomes: Memoirs of a Most Respectable Family, edited by Arthur Pendennis, Esq.*

1854   *The Rose and the Ring, or the History of Prince Giglio and Prince Bulbo: A Fireside Pantomime for Great and Small Children*

1857–9   *The Virginians: A Tale of the Last Century*

1860   *The Four Georges: Sketches of Manners, Morals,*
            Court, and Town Life (lectures delivered 1855)
            Lovel the Widower
1861–2   *The Adventures of Philip on His Way through the*
            World; Shewing Who Robbed Him, Who Helped
            Him, and Who Passed Him By
1864   *Denis Duval* (unfinished)

The editions used in the present work for the purpose of quotation
are as follows :

  Henry Esmond : Harmondsworth, Middx : Penguin Books, 1970.
  Edited by J. Sutherland and M. Greenfield.
  Vanity Fair : Boston : Houghton Mifflin, Riverside Editions,
  1962; London : Methuen, 1963. Edited by Geoffrey and
  Kathleen Tillotson.
For all other Thackeray works quoted : *The Oxford Thackeray*,
edited by George Saintsbury, London, 1912.